Don't Think Less of Me

Don't Think Less of Me

A collection of essays

Tim O'Shea

First Paperback Edition

Grateful acknowledgement is made to Maureen O'Connell of the *Concord Journal* and to Rachel Morton, former Editor of *Middlebury Magazine* in which some of these essays were first published. Additional debt of gratitude is owed to Gary Waleik and Bill Littlefield of National Public Radio's "Only a Game." Many thanks to Cassandra Hiland for her advice, direction, and patience. Finally, a big shout-out to Big Fist McClung, wherever you are.

Library of Congress Cataloguing-in-Publication Data
O'Shea, Tim.
      Don't Think Less of Me: A Collection of Essays / by Tim
      O'Shea. – 1ˢᵗ ed.
      ISBN 1-4196-2978-6 (pb)

Cover photo courtesy of Sam O'Shea

Comments at comments@lastdrop.org

To KOS, SOS and MOS

BATTERIES NOT INCLUDED

MY daughter is confident we're getting a dog any day now, but I don't have the heart to tell her we can't. I'm sorry she'll never feel the joy of holding a new puppy or the excitement of seeing a hamster make its first run on the exercise wheel, but I'm doing her a favor. You can't out-swim your gene pool, and her daddy's end is too deep for any pet to tread water. You see, her daddy comes from a long line of pet killers.

It never should have been this way. We were a nice family, a little short on brainpower and patience, perhaps, but not the kind of folk you'd look at in church and think, softly, to yourself, "Murderers." Sadly, though, the record states otherwise. As far back as I can remember, we had pets in the house. We loved the thrill of getting a new animal and the promise the moment would bring. Yes, *getting* pets was easy for us; keeping them alive was where we struggled. The killing time started innocently enough. When I was around five or six, we had a guinea pig we kept caged in my room. I'd fall asleep each night to the sounds of Butterscotch trying to claw its way to freedom, and I imagined a career as a zookeeper or a lion tamer, thinking if I was the one tasked with watching this beast, someone must have seen promise in me. That promise would be short-lived.

One morning I awoke to trouble. Butterscotch was in distress, lying on his side, his big dark eyes rolling back in his head. I screamed for help, and my brother and two sisters bolted into the room, quickly followed by our mother, who arrived, sized up the situation, and announced, "This animal is choking on a cedar shaving! Quick! Get my tweezers!"

My sister ran to fetch them as my mom lifted the rodent from its cage, squeezed its mouth open at the jaw line, and peered in as we circled in wonder around her. My sister returned with the tweezers, handed them to my mom and joined the witness pool. "Yup," my mom said casually, as if she'd done this before. "Choking on a cedar shaving, that's all." She reached in with the metal pincers, grabbed hold and yanked out hard and fast. Butterscotch let out what sounded like the whine from a small engine as my mom held aloft what she thought was the cedar shaving. But it didn't look like a cedar shaving – it looked like a tiny tongue. My god! It *was* a tiny tongue – Butterscotch's tongue! We screamed in horror at the sight of our dead pet, and my mom screamed as she realized she held a dead member of the rat family in her hands; and, well, Butterscotch, he didn't really scream as much as he gurgled a bit, and then he hushed up pretty quickly.

This, it turns out, was not the first murder in our house. A few years before the Tweezer Incident, my sister Molly foreshadowed most of our pets' destiny. Molly had won the chance to care for her pre-school's pet guinea pig over a long weekend, and in an effort to demonstrate her undying love and devotion, my sister hugged the mascot to death – squeezed the life right out of it, whispering as she clenched, "I love him so much! I love him so much!" which might explain why her new husband always seems a bit skittish around her.

My mother's and sister's deftness at petricide awakened a latent bloodlust in the family, because the mishaps continued as we grew. Truth be told, we were guilty of bad judgment, I think, more than outright murder. For instance, we once owned two rabbits, male and female, really nice ones - quite fluffy and well groomed. We kept them in a fancy hutch in our yard, with a screened-in porch and shag carpeting on the inside walls. However, we never bothered to figure out if they were brother and sister or boyfriend and girlfriend; we just chucked them into the doublewide deluxe and got back to *Mutual of Omaha's Wild Kingdom with Marlin Perkins* on the TV.

A few weeks later we learned our rabbits were up to the devil's business in the doublewide when we spied a heap of squirming little bunnies in the sawdust. We thought the father would eat the babies, so we promptly removed him - at least we thought it was the father. Either way, it didn't really matter because, for all we knew, mommy rabbits ate their young just as much as the daddies did. We were just playing the odds.

The next morning we discovered our backyard Miracle of Life had quickly transformed itself into the Chamber of Death. The remaining parent had done his/her best to erase all evidence of recent fornication by eating each and every one of his/her babies. It didn't take long for my parents to sour on the idea that we were harboring baby-eating sex addicts on our property, so we got rid of the rabbits, leaving them to run free on a golf course a few blocks away. I saw one of the bunnies a few years later, but the contempt in his/her eyes warned me to keep my distance.

I tried keeping hamsters, only to find that bringing defenseless woodland creatures into a house thoroughly dominated by two experienced, free-roaming cats was a lousy idea. None of the hamsters lasted more than three weeks. I found Mr. Bill's head on the stairs one morning; a second, Bonzo, got away from the cats, escaping down the radiator on the third floor. We could hear its feeble scratches for help from behind the mirror in my parents' bathroom for a day or so until Bonzo succumbed to the asbestos, most likely.

We had lots of cats. One cat, White Kitty, was run over by my mom's friend in the driveway. Another, Brown Kitty, sprinted away one sunny summer morning, apparently figuring she ought to get out while she had all her faculties.

We had a few other cats beat the odds and live a long life as family pets, despite serious brushes with death. Copy Cat had a habit of napping on the folded section of our raised garage door, at least until the day my mom closed the door and drove off to get me at school. As we drove up the driveway, we saw Copy Cat hanging from the upper section of the closed garage door, her paws stuck in the door's fold. We approached, and Copy Cat, suspended and powerless, turned her head slightly and let out a whimpering "meow," which, translated into English, probably meant, "You careless bastards." I lifted the bottom of the door, and Copy Cat fell to the ground and limped around on what looked like huge cat clown feet, her throbbing front paws flattened and misshapen. She darted off into the bushes as my mom and I thanked our stars for little victories.

We lost so many pets we stopped naming them after a while. My mom and dad would arrive home from the animal shelter, a new dog in tow. We'd run expectantly to the door. "What's its name?" we'd holler, and my parents would get that pained look of resignation on their faces, like the slaughterhouse owners bringing a pig home for the weekend, muttering, "Say, let's give this young fella a chance to get acquainted before we name him. Whaddaya say?" What we should have said was, "Run, Sprinkles, run! Run as if your life depends on it – because it does!" Instead, we'd stare at each other, put some newspaper down and get back to the TV, waiting for the dog to find himself in enough trouble for us to make hasty funeral arrangements.

We had Esther the dog – killed by a car; Casey, a true housedog – killed by a local gang of tough dogs. We even had Butkus, who lasted for seven calendar days before realizing what was going on and taking off faster than I've ever seen another dog run since. Smart dog.

And then there was Tucker, a dog with a heartbeat so irregular that he was something of a medical marvel. Our neighbor, Dr. Allen Ahearn, or as we called him out of earshot, "Doctor Al the Puppy's Pal," once listened to Tucker's oddly beating chest and begged us to let him operate on the dog, "for the sake of veterinary science." He promised to increase Tucker's lifespan for a mere $10,000. We passed on the idea, more out of respect for the dog's privacy than for the hefty price tag, and Tucker ended up outliving all predictions, his heart step-dancing to its own spastic drumbeat for years and years.

He finally found enough rhythm to impregnate the neighbors' purebred golden retriever, who'd been previously segregated from the ranks of the unclean dogs for the purpose of starting its own little master race of uber-puppies. Our neighbors were so infuriated they had Doctor Al abort the puppies, denying Tucker his one true chance of living on in the bloodline of his mongrel offspring. Sadly, even when our pets helped usher life into the world, death quickly followed.

When Tucker's end came, it was no less dramatic. He died of a massive heart attack on the kitchen floor, only to revive himself enough to loosen his bowels, drop dead fifteen seconds later and then, like a four-legged Lazarus, arise in the back seat of the car en route to the dog emergency room. Then things got ugly. While pacing in the waiting room, Tucker collapsed dead at my brother Mike's feet. He and my mom carried Tucker's lifeless body into the exam room where Doctor Al's protégé awaited. The protégé informed them that, yes, Tucker had died, and as my mom left the room to iron out the funeral details, the good doctor shocked Tucker back to life with a doggy defibrillator, making it two round trips from death to life in the span of thirty minutes.

The vet then announced that Tucker had suffered a stroke and would never again have full bladder control or the use of his hind legs and offered us a simple, final solution. We took it, but not before being charged $350 for the death, rebirth, death and final burial of the dog. All things considered, we probably should have spent the $10,000 for Tucker's operation, at least to avoid the drama. And as Tucker's soul floated towards pet heaven, I imagined a tongueless rodent flapping its angel wings in vengeful glee.

I pray my daughter forgives me for not sharing her enthusiasm for a family pet, but it's my job to save her from certain disappointment. Besides, Santa brought her a "Furr-Real" Cat this past Christmas, a battery-powered, hair-covered, life-sized kitty that purrs and hisses on command. It's really the ideal solution – once Furr-Real stops making noise, a nifty swap of the batteries quickly brings her back to life. I shudder to think how many cats, dogs, fish, gerbils, hamsters and bunnies would still be with us if they'd only come with batteries. It would have made things much easier on all of us.

HALLOWEEN IS HELL

WHEN I think of Halloween, I am reminded of four things – assault, battery, racial discord and urine-soaked buckskin chaps. Any one of those can ruin a holiday, but combine them, and I vote for a cancellation of the whole damn thing. "What kind of person are you?" you're probably asking right now. "What kind of parent yearns for a Halloween-free October?" I do. I suffered through many Halloweens in my youth, and I figured once I was of voting age, I was in the clear. No such luck. It got no better, and now, as a parent, Halloween is relentless, spreading its misery around like a wanton trick-or-treater flinging razor-filled apples into the crowd.

I've tried to warn my kids about the

horrors of Halloween, but they'll have none of it. I try to relate some of my experiences to scare them off, but they won't budge. "Kids will beat you up!" I say as my son pries another Juju Be from his molars. "They'll all laugh and point at you," I scream as my daughter lobs Sweet Tarts into her brother's mouth. "You'll wet your pants and they'll make you dress like a savage," I'll yell, and that's when they get up and walk out to check on the status of their outfits.

My earliest memory of Halloween didn't have much to do with the actual holiday – it had more to do with the costume. I was a student in a neighborhood preschool, and from the first day there, I was filled with a sense of dread and fear whenever the idea of dressing up was mentioned, for tucked away in a back room sat the Costume Box! The school rule was that if we got too messy from paint, dirt or our own fecal matter, we'd be dragged into the back room for an appointment with the Costume Box.

The costumes covered all genres. There were princesses, knights, sailors, nurses, pilots, pirates and cowboys, and every day someone would be transformed into one of these, no matter how stalwart the resistance. I was the neatest kid for seven months, chuckling to myself whenever a classmate grew careless with the finger-paint and ended up looking like one of the Village People. I made sure I capped all the paint properly and never walked too close to the hyper kid during magic marker hour, and I always remembered to eat my snacks with delicate caution.

One morning I'd spent so much time worrying about staying clean that I forgot to make it to the bathroom in time. I peed all over myself, soaking my corduroys. I burst into tears, not so much from the lack of bladder control, but more from the fate awaiting me in the back room - the Costume Box! The teachers hustled me into the room and took my measurements. I lobbied hard for Pip the Pirate, thinking the eye patch would distract the kids from noticing I wasn't wearing any underpants. But no! The teachers had grander designs – buckskin Indian chaps and an elk-bone chest plate. They contemplated war paint but figured my tears would make it run. The worst part was, and I remember them laughing so hard they couldn't breathe, was the full-feathered headdress. This was pre-*Dances With Wolves,* and I'm sure they toyed with the idea of splashing some settler blood on the lapels for the full "red demon of the Great Plains" effect. Thankfully, cooler heads prevailed, but for the entire day I looked like Cochise's chubby nephew. I tried to force out some more urine to make a case for the pirate suit, but it really didn't matter. All I knew was that I'd been scarred for life and didn't want any costumes in my future.

My first experience with the ritual donning of costumes for Halloween took place in kindergarten. My mom coerced me into wearing a dime-store devil costume. It was a non-breathable vinyl devil's coat and a mask of Satan himself, complete with two tiny red horns that lit up at the press of a button. As we headed to the school bus, my sisters ran ahead and must have said something, because the entire busload of kids, in unison, ran to the side of the bus and started laughing. I got so nervous that I pressed the horns' button again and again and again, which made the kids laugh even harder, sending me running home in tears, a pint-sized Satan humbled in front of his minions. I should have known things would not improve.

So traumatized was I by the wholesale Rejection of Satan that I avoided Halloween completely until I was peer-pressured into dressing like a homeless man as a twelve-year old. My friends were fixated on the laziest Halloween costume next to the eyes-cut-out-of-a-sheet ghost look – the Bum. The Bum, or classic American Hobo, is a Halloween favorite, consisting of a ratty shirt or sweatshirt, tattered or mud-caked pants, and a crazy hat, usually an old bowler or stained sunbonnet. We'd take a cork, burn the end and smear our faces with it, just enough to give us that cartoonish five o'clock shadow style favored by the bums on TV. We were going for the railyard-tramp-of-yesteryear look, but we ended up like a squad of midget Emmett Kellys, wandering from door to door in search of the perfect popcorn ball. Apparently our understanding of the homeless issue was a bit off as well; what we should have done was add a squeegee tool and a rag bucket to the outfit for verisimilitude, but off we went.

Armed only with our charcoal-smudged faces and a few pillowcases, we spent the night bartering and cajoling for candy from every house in town. After a few hours, our bags bulged with booty as we struggled down the street. If there's an easier mark out there than a pack of pre-teen bums wandering down the poorly lit street, lugging pounds of candy and fruit, I'd like to see it.

With three blocks to go before the end of the night, a group of kids jumped us. I don't remember much except getting hit and tossed to the ground. As I rolled over on my back, a girl a few years older than me was on top, slapping me back and forth across the head, knocking my derby aside, screaming, "Give it up, little boy! Give it up!" I did what any pudgy sixth grader holding $35 worth of stale candy would do – I took my lumps and held onto that bag for dear life.

Finally, my assailant grew tired of thumping me and gave up, as she and her cohorts ran off into the night. I sat up and smiled, knowing we'd won, only to find that my friends had surrendered their candy at the first sign of trouble. Despite being the last tramp standing, I couldn't decide which was more painful – getting my ass thoroughly kicked by an 8th grade girl or having to share my loot with three friends.

After the Hobo Beatdown, I spent the next few years trick-or-treating with a grudge. I'd collect my fair share of candy but focused more on the UNICEF donations. I'd outfit myself with five or six little orange boxes and collect quite a bit of cash, never turning in a cent to the proper UN authorities. All Saints' Day would roll around, and my pockets would jingle with the weight of ill-gotten charity gains. The way I saw it, Halloween owed me for that beating a few years before, and I was getting what was mine.

By the time I'd made it to college, I'd distanced myself from the holiday, figuring costumes were but a distant memory. I was wrong, but at least this time, I got to sit back and watch Halloween rear its ugly pumpkin head at someone else.

Two months into my college experience, my roommate, John, had what he thought was a brilliant idea. He dressed up like Clarence Clemmons from the E Street Band, complete with red beret and tiny saxophone. John was one of the whitest people I'd ever met – in fact, his freckles gave him more of an orange hue than anything, prompting him to choose blackface makeup to round out the costume. He spent hours getting ready, dabbing a little paint here, shifting his beret a bit there, all the while bragging how this was the best costume he'd ever worn. "It's so real! I look just like him!" he kept saying between gulps of beer.

Finally, it was Showtime. John emerged from our basement room, oblivious to the reality that our dorm was, at that exact moment, hosting Minority Recruitment weekend, and as he strode into the Common Room, holding the toy horn in his white-gloved hands, John looked around, paused, and realized he was surrounded by two dozen black students, each of whom stared in dumbfounded amazement. John lost his beret in the ensuing scramble back downstairs, and as he tried in vain to coax a few bars of "Dancing in the Dark" out of his plastic saxophone, I explained to him the many horrors of Halloween. At least now I had a witness to the truth, a cohort in my hatred for the holiday.

There's been little improvement since that night long ago. Many Halloweens have come and gone, and nothing's gotten better. As a parent, I've had to confront Halloween head-on in hopes that my distaste would discourage my kids from participating. But I've had no luck. Our son's in grade school, and the Halloween conversations begin in summertime. This summer, we got stuck on a *Star Wars* theme, my son believing that the perfect costume would take months of planning. I held enough sway to convince him that a Space Mollusk costume from the nightclub scene in *Attack of the Clones* wasn't easy to find, although the image of a cephalopod hopping from door to door begging for mini Clark bars had some potential.

Many times my wife and I have been forced to listen to our son's sermons on the curative powers of nougat. And it's like this every year. For us, Halloween season begins in late May and runs until mid-winter, when the children finally have to outrun the congealed mass of Swedish Fish lurking in the basement laundry room, like the Blob looking for careless teenagers at the local diner.

But I refuse to join them in their pursuit of the perfect costume. Sure, I'll fund their efforts and may even slap on a few extra rolls of aluminum foil on next year's Robot, but I'll be damned if I'm getting dressed up again. I admit to owning a large dog costume and have even attended a few costume parties in the last few years, but I blame alcohol for those indiscretions. Besides, the lingering fear of wetting my pants or getting jumped at the door is enough to give me pause. The sad truth is that I resent Halloween – I resent the happy faces, the confident choosing of costumes, the careless disregard for dental hygiene.

This resentment isn't going anywhere. I have a ways to go before I can put this nightmare to rest. My kids love Halloween, and I see no end to the costume hunts, the nonstop stream of wrappers, and the ringing doorbells. But one day, who knows when, I'll be rid of Halloween, and my world will be a better place. And at that point, I'll buy my own candy.

WHO'S THE BLACK SHEEP?

Every family has a black sheep. Like your cousin, the red-haired kid who began his toast at your aunt's wedding, "A feminist rabbi, a French monkey and a talking salami walk into a bar," or your kid sister you saw on CNN during the NAFTA riots. ("Is that Mary with the nipple ring and flare gun?") The black sheep isn't the one who ignites his farts on command or burps The Lord's Prayer - it's the one whose behavior disrupts the entire family dynamic.

When I was a kid, I had no chance to be the black sheep in my family. My older siblings did their best to seize that crown, jockeying to outdo each other every chance they got. There were nights they'd arrive at the dinner table together, grinning from ear to ear, and I was panicked they'd just hatched the next day's diabolical plan. It turns out they were smiling from the high-quality hemp they'd just smoked in my brother's attic bedroom, but I was convinced I was eating dinner with apprentice members of the Legion of Doom.

I'd sit at the table, riveted by the sordid details my mother would recount to my dad of what one of her children had done that day to earn the dark badge of dysfunction. Secretly, I'd wonder when it'd be my turn, when I'd have the guts to attempt some of the stunts they'd pulled with such panache. There was the time Dan got into a fistfight with his 8th grade science teacher, or the time my sister Kara snuck out to spend the night playing Spin the Malt Liquor Bottle on the golf course, or the time Molly got hit by a car while cutting class. Being the black sheep in my family was serious business, and I feared I wasn't up to the challenge.

My earliest memory of the family black sheep is the infamous Applesauce Oreo Tin Toss Battle Royale of 1977. Dan, the eldest, was something of a mystery; he played the piano and was obsessed with Billy Joel, and he'd spend hours with his buddies in one of many tree houses they'd built around town. I had no idea that tree houses were perfect for pill popping and glue sniffing, and I bet the lilting sounds of Billy Joel's music threw the adults off the scent of trouble. "Sing us the song, you're the Piano Man," guzzle guzzle snort snort. . .

One night, my glassy-eyed brother tried to pour himself a tall glass of orange juice as we sat down for dinner. Dan had lots of wacky ideas about beverages. He once tried to make hard cider in his room, but the mason jars eventually exploded like grenades, blasting half-fermented apple cider and glass shrapnel across his bedroom. He also held to the theory that orange juice tasted better if poured from an elevation. He'd raise the pitcher as high above the glass as he could and pour away, proclaiming, "This gives the juice a chance to attract more oxygen," a strategy he must have picked up from his paint-thinner parties.

Well, on this night, the glass was too small or the bennies were starting to kick in, but either way it didn't matter because he missed the glass spectacularly, pouring the juice onto the counter. My mother, mixing a just-finished pot of applesauce, already cranky from keeping five hungry kids at bay, yelled, "Dammit! You did that on purpose!"

Dan, with pride hurt and pupils dilated, replied, "On purpose? I'll give you something on purpose!" and he poured the remainder of the orange juice all over the counter and onto the floor. Quick as a cornered bobcat, my mom flung a wooden spoon across the kitchen, aiming for her son but smashing the empty juice pitcher to pieces.

Relentless in her rage, she picked up a cast-iron frying pan and whacked Dan in the butt. Clutching his rump, Dan screamed, "Sic Semper Tyrannis," I think, or maybe it was "Kiss My Grits." It really didn't matter because in one grand sweep of his rugby-shirted forearm, Dan whipped the still-simmering vat of applesauce against the wall, grabbed the Oreo tin and announced, "Now *this*! *This* is on purpose!" and he dumped the Oreos into the mass of smushed, warm apples and ran out of the house before my mother could butterfly him like a rack of lamb.

Dan hopped on his Huffy 3-Speed and headed for the closest tree house to cool his heels for a few days, nursing his wounds with side B of *Turnstiles* and the solace that my dad had missed the whole show, bedridden with a slipped disc, unable to lend either a stern hand or a steady mop to the situation downstairs. The mop became irrelevant as our dog Esther happily gorged herself on all the free eats. Soon after, she barfed up every morsel on the white Persian rug in the dining room.

I was sure that Dan had locked up the family black sheep distinction with that effort for good, but I was wrong.

In junior high school, my sister Molly set fire to a trashcan during chorus rehearsal; apparently another rousing version of "The Cat Came Back" was too much for her. She claimed she did it by accident, which prompted us to wonder what does a thirteen-year old kid do on *purpose* with a Bic lighter other than set fire to stuff?

Dan's pathologies and Molly's dalliances were fun to witness, but neither measured up to the multi-year repeat black sheep run my sister Kara put together in the late 70's and early 80's. Kara reigned as the O'Shea black sheep for years, out-doing all comers with her nose for trouble and a wanton disregard for the laws of physics. Her efforts bewildered our parents. If there was ice to fall through in wintertime, Kara was on it. If there were parties to be had while my parents were away, Kara was hosting. If there was a sixer to drain and a pack of smokes to enjoy before homeroom, Kara was buying.

She had an aura about her, a swagger that terrified and mesmerized me. Once during dinner at our summerhouse, my mom marched forth from the kitchen with a freshly baked pie, only to stumble and drop it on the floor. We laughed like hyenas until my dad demanded we stop. Only Kara kept laughing, and then bolted from the table when my dad screamed at her. She ran down to the dock, hopped into the canoe, paddled thirty feet offshore, and sat there defiant.

Knowing our dad could swim like a bag of lug nuts added to her genius choice of getaway vessel, and from that point on, I knew I could never compete for black sheep status with Kara around.

When she was seventeen, Kara was hired to baby-sit for a wealthy Manhattan family for the last few weeks of the summer. The family vacationed in the Hamptons, at the famed Maidstone Country Club. Kara lasted three days before tucking the kids in bed, stealing the family's station wagon, and using the tee box on the 10th hole of their country club's golf course to launch her homage to Evil Knievel's Snake Canyon rocket car jump. Kara landed in a sand trap with a busted-up station wagon and took a trip to the local hoosegow in handcuffs. My dad rescued her soon after, managing not only to retrieve the original mug shots but also to get all records wiped clean as well. I have a dim memory of being hustled into the car for an impromptu trip out of state until, as my sister whispered to me, "the heat cools off." How could I compete with that?

A few years before Kara's failed moon launch, my mom was at her wits' end. Kara had been through a rough stretch, including a spectacular double-expulsion in one school year. She'd managed to get booted from our town's public high school, only to be sent off to a Catholic girls' school nearby, then to be summarily dismissed from there as well months later, arriving back in the public school, bowed but unbent.

My mom asked if I thought the nurses had switched babies on her in the hospital. For a second, I thought she was berating me for not shouldering my black sheep burden equally, but I glanced at my sister's mug shots in the glove compartment and realized I was off the hook. I almost agreed with my mom about the switched infants, considering the mounting evidence against Kara, but I hoped my time would come and let the question go unanswered.

Even Mike, the youngest, had his moment before I did, and he was barely out of diapers. One winter evening, my mom and dad sat down to enjoy dinner, and just as my dad cracked open another Carling Black Label, my mom realized she was out of gin. She did what any self-respecting socially drinking mother of five would do – she dialed up her neighbor across the street and begged for any spare booze, bathtub or otherwise.

Off Mike went to fetch the bottle. On his return, he slipped on the icy sidewalk and broke his fall with the brimming bottle of gin, cut his hand, soaked his snorkel jacket, and ruined my parents' plans for the evening.

Nassau County's Social Service system was not quite as thorough back then, so my parents skated through the emergency room process, never once asked to explain why their wounded preschooler was pickled in cheap booze. Rumor has it the social worker reminded my parents of the flexibility of plastic, but the damage had been done.

Looking back, I'm not sure who is more to blame for this episode - Mike for dropping the gin, my dad for failing to shovel the sidewalk, or my mom for relying on neighbors for alcohol when there was plenty of cooking sherry and Witch Hazel in the house. Considering such an event would now land my parents in Family Court, I think all three of them may have shared the black sheep award for that performance.

My time finally came, ages after most of us had moved out of the house and on to other things. For years I never had the guts to pull something off like my older siblings. The only place I threw Oreos was down my throat, and the only fires I set were properly supervised. In fact, the one episode that finally gave me notoriety, however fleeting, was more black schlep than black sheep. But it was finally my time to shine, and shine I did.

My moment in the black light began innocently enough on the night before Thanksgiving. I'd graduated from college the spring before and headed out for the night. A friendly cold beer with a few buddies, soon followed by a few more, quickly rounded out by a series of vodka shots, a funnel or two to balance things a bit, a cigarette to kill the beer taste, and three or four spritzers to erase any semblance of sobriety, and the next thing I know, I'm lying flat in the trunk of my buddy Sean's car, listening to him beg the cop to let him get me home.

Thanksgiving dawn arrived, and my mom greeted me with a loud, "Good morning!" I responded immediately with "Good Christ! I think I'm gonna hurl," which led my baster-wielding mother to banish me from the house until I "got my act together." I hid in the back of my sister's broken-down car until I made a dash for freedom, tripped and was quickly covered with leaves by my brother Mike and his leaf blower.

I stayed there for a few hours, alternating between dry heaving and making leaf angels on the lawn. I managed to sneak inside for Thanksgiving dinner, only to be shamed to the basement by my seventy-five-year-old great aunt, who was convinced I was going to get everyone sick with The Grippe.

As I slouched towards the basement, my mother screamed, "Dammit! He ruined Thanksgiving!" My bile-filled body swelled with pride - for a few shining hours I alone wore the O'Shea black sheep crown, not an insignificant thing in my family. As I lay on the basement floor, the cool tiles calming my tortured belly, I fell into a blissful sleep, lulled by my siblings' laughter from the dining room table above, confident I'd risen to the challenge. I could finally say I was somebody. I belonged. I was a black sheep too.

KNOW ANY GOOD BABYSITTERS?

It wasn't until my brother finally lit the gasoline, dancing a jig as the flames leapt toward the sky, that I realized baby-sitting was a dangerous business. I was six or seven and had seen my share of sitters by then. But I hadn't yet seen fire introduced into the equation until my brother Danny, a seventh grader with a penchant for the dramatic, ignited the driveway. Mrs. Sharkey, the latest in a parade of short-tempered, underpaid sitters, was the target of his attack. Her crime was to refuse my brother the right take the family station wagon out for a ride on the Jones Beach Causeway.

Naturally, Danny responded as any middle-schooler with access to gasoline and an audience would do – he poured the fuel down the length of our U-shaped driveway, screamed some Blue Oyster Cult lyrics, and dropped the match to the ground. He wasn't really trying to hurt anyone.

He was just reminding Mrs. Sharkey who was really the boss in my parents' absence.

My dad's job required him to spend a lot of time away from home. My mother joined him as often as she could, meaning we were left with strange women quite a bit. These were not the four-hour variety - the high school kid from down the block with braces and a sack full of homework – no, these were battle-hardened matrons who looked and dressed like models from the pages of *Prison Guard Quarterly*. Lord knows where my parents found them, but they'd all arrive with the same take-charge air and gruff demeanor, convinced that these soft, spoiled kids would be no match for their years of church-going and clean living. They were wrong – my older siblings smelled weakness like hornets smelled fear, and each sitter ended up on the losing end of a battle they never knew they were fighting.

My clearest memory of one, Mrs. Bell, was of her washing dishes in scalding hot water with a smile on her face. I asked her how she did it, and she turned, the grin draining from her face, saying, "God only burns the sinners," prompting me to get down on my knees that night and pray for my parents' swift return. She put up quite a front, but the moment my parents arrived, Mrs. Bell broke into sobs of pain, declaring she'd never work for us again. She got her wish and dropped dead of a heart attack two weeks later. God must have needed another angel in His kitchen because we sure were done with her.

After a while, my parents must have realized that there was zero repeat business. I imagine they resorted to posting leaflets at the bus station, their theory being that a pulse and a general idea of how to open a box of frozen waffles was good enough to qualify for the job.

As for Mrs. Sharkey, she never came back after my brother's driveway pyrotechnics demonstration, and I bet she slept with a hammer under her pillow for the month it took for my parents to return from Australia.

She was quickly followed by the Macrobiotic Baby-sitters for my parents' next trip. Fresh off the commune, these two freaks floated in with bags of bean curd, sacks of brown rice, and their little baby Ethan, who was allergic to everything in our house. Television was off limits, sugar cereals were banned, and cookies, cakes and ice cream, signs of ugly living, were similarly out of reach. Without *The Gong Show*, Ring Dings and Cocoa Krispies, our house was like a Hutterite homestead without the farm equipment and hair bonnets.

Ethan got all the attention, which was fine for my siblings, but not for me. They'd be out front firing bottle rockets at cars, and I'd be stuck inside wrestling with Baby Ethan for a handful of chick peas, wondering when in the hell my parents were getting home so we could turn on the damn TV.

Lousy baby-sitting relationships are a time-tested tradition in my family. My dad had a German nanny at the outbreak of World War II who was hired while my grandparents left town for a few weeks. Right after the attack on Pearl Harbor, she locked my dad in his room and fed him Romaine lettuce under the door until his parents returned home days later. My grandparents fired the German sitter and hired a Japanese-American couple who'd been dealing with its own internment in the California desert. Harry and Joyce Kiuchi worked for my dad's family until Harry hit the bottle, and, after mixing three quarts of sake-spiked eggnog and a few judo moves, he crashed into the family Christmas tree, ruining the holidays and getting himself fired in the process.

As suspect as they were at choosing sitters, my parents did a pretty rough job of rearing sitters as well. Soon after Mrs. Bell's demise, Danny and my sisters were put in charge. Being baby-sat by my older siblings was like wearing a Piggy costume at a *Lord of the Flies* keg party. Their favorite game was to chase me down and hang me by my underwear in the linen closet, the rule being I could come down once the elastic snapped, which it did every single time.

Even my spiritual health was put at risk, often by my siblings' love of pizza. Their plan was to have our dad drop us off at church, breeze in the back for a glimpse of the priest and an inkling of the day's gospel, and then hightail it out of there in search of a few slices and some garlic knots at the Italian Kitchen around the corner. I will admit, though, that choosing between eternal salvation and a hot slice of Sicilian is still a tough call for me.

Once my little brother Mike arrived, things heated up considerably. When Mike was an infant, Danny and my sisters took swift advantage of the situation. They'd hide Mike in the closet, take the biggest doll they could find and overturn the crib with the doll's head pinned underneath the crib's railing. They'd scream and dart into the closet as my mom ran upstairs to rescue her infant son. My siblings would then burst forth from the closet, Mike still sleeping in their arms, laughing like they'd just pulled the funniest prank in the book. Come to think of it, maybe that's why my parents left the house so often. With kids like that, who wanted quality family time?

At other times my siblings were just careless. Our basement stairs, the steepest in the house, were right off the kitchen. Mike would wheel around the kitchen in his walker like AJ Foyt at Indy until one night my sister Kara left the basement door open. Although we were never allowed to recreate the event, we swore that Mike and his walker did one full flip before coming to rest at the foot of the stairs. Lucky for my sister, the walker took the brunt of the damage. Another time, Mike got his head stuck between the spindles of a footstool – and to this day my sisters swear that learning to use a jigsaw under pressure is really the best way.

Mike's entry into this world had been an issue for me – in 1975, I was nine years old and had a firm hold on my parents' attention. I vaguely remember them discussing the idea of adopting a Vietnamese boat baby, and I was terrified, convinced that this baby would bring part of that "ongoing gorilla war" I'd seen on TV into our house. The image of a rifle-toting baby monkey terrified me, and I was thrilled when my parents changed their minds.

A few months later, they gathered us around the dinner table to explain that they "had news for the family."

This stands as the only time my family has ever gathered 'round the table for a family chat. I had a better chance of hearing what my family's plans were from the mailman than I did from them – we just weren't that kind of family.

Nonetheless, my parents succeeded in corralling us long enough to announce that we would soon have another family member. I panicked, envisioning nightly gun battles with my new baby brother, Bao Tran the killer ape, but my mom quickly explained that she was pregnant. My brother and sisters smiled in a slightly off-kilter way, but I wasn't smiling. I knew that one day I'd be called upon to baby-sit, a daunting thought based on the violence, neglect, and cruelty I witnessed weekly at the hands of sitters, blood relations included.

Babysitting Mike was hell – he'd turned out just like the rest of my siblings, and he knew I was weak. He'd heard about the repeated emasculations during my trips to Linen Closet Wedgieville. Armed with that information and a vague sense of what it took to survive in our house, Mike had enough chutzpah to hold me at bay until my parents came home every time I watched him.

His favorite move was the sneak attack. He once clocked me with a candlestick, creeping up behind me and whacking me silly. Instead of reprimanding him, I ran for my life, hiding in the kitchen. The kitchen was often no safer. One night, after repeated arguments over the dinner menu, Mike cornered me and attacked, biting me in the belly, insistent that I give him the bologna. As I tried to stem the blood flow, Mike grabbed the lunchmeat and scampered off into the house like the escaped primate I suspected he really was.

Mike was a mild-mannered kid, but there was something about those baby-sitting shifts that brought out the meanness in him. It could have been the simian blood, or the smell of processed meats, or the fact that our house never had capable baby-sitters. For a while I assumed he'd taken a bigger whack on the head from his fall down the stairs than we originally thought, but in the end, Mike grew up like the rest of us and figured there were smarter things to do than attack the child-care provider or set fire to the driveway.

I have two kids of my own, and I'm always on the lookout for suspicious signs when we leave them with sitters. Are there pellet guns handy? Where's the gas for the lawn mower? What are chick peas anyway, and are there any in the house? As it turns out, my kids seem pretty normal, at least until we announce our childfree six-week European vacation next summer. Mrs. Sharkey won't return my calls, so if you have any ideas, let me know.

EXIT THE DRAGON

There are three things I really fear in this world: flying insects, really hot French onion soup, and Patrick Heaney, not necessarily in that order. Flying bugs need no explanation, and as for French Onion soup, that bowl of molten cheese, oily brown broth and twice-cooked onions is like a tiny serving of hell.

As I've gotten older, I've been able to get a handle on the insect issue, and I've developed a fondness for gazpacho, but the mention of Patrick Heaney's name still causes my sphincters to clench with dread. Pat was my best friend Sean's older brother, and he may have been the most evil person I ever saw up close.

Pat wasn't a bully by any stretch. On the surface, he appeared to be a nice boy – pleasant smile, affable nature, nicely coiffed reddish dreadlocks – just what you'd expect from an Irish-American suburban kid. But beneath the smile lurked the heart of a fiend. Pat delighted in torment, not so much of his little brother, Sean, but of his brother's friends, which, for a while, meant me and me alone. Living a few houses down the street from the Heaneys made me Pat's pint-sized private punching bag for most of my formative years.

Pat was no dummy; he is, in fact, one of the smartest people I've ever met, not in the "Let's split atoms in the basement" kind of way, but more in the "How can I manipulate this 8-year old kid into amusing me and barfing up his lunch in the process?" kind of way.

Pat delighted in elaborate torture schemes, each one beginning with the promise of friendship but ending in sore ribs, red ears, and muffled tears. He hatched his plans under the pretense of looking out for his kid brother, a ploy that won some approval from Sean but endless misery for me. As I look back, Sean must have been overjoyed as I rode my three-speed bike up his driveway, my third-grade face filled with the promise of a bruise-free visit; Sean knew better, hiding like Boo Radley in the curtains as Pat finalized the details of his latest plan, knowing I was too dumb and too slow to realize what awaited me as I walked through the door.

I spent hours at Sean's house, most of it fearing Pat was lurking behind the recliner or in the Heaney's expansive food closet. Pat was the first kid I ever saw skateboard, wear Converse High Tops, use a snowboard, affix a gas mask to a bong, and eat cereal from a soup tureen. I knew I should have run away as fast as possible, but I couldn't. Watching him was like watching a garage on fire – you know it's bad and you know someone could get hurt, but that gas can could blow at any time and make a really cool noise with fire and stuff. The problem was that I was usually the one getting blown up, but still I was mesmerized.

We could usually follow a trail of spilled cereal to find Pat munching away in front of the TV; just seeing him sitting on the couch with a salad bowl full of Cookie Crisp cereal and a few cans of Fanta Orange filled me with awe and a healthy measure of fear. He looked like bad news just staring at the television, doing nothing but laughing like Cookie Jarvis as Dee, Rerun and Roger got ready for the Doobie Brothers concert.

The torment started harmlessly enough. I was seven years old and looking forward to my first sleepover. Off I went with my carefully packed bag, which included a flashy new Chinese silk robe my parents had brought me from their recent trip to Hong Kong. I couldn't wait to show that robe off – it was brown and gold, with a fire-breathing dragon on the back. We had some pizza and then it was into pajamas (and fancy robe, if you had one). Up to this point, Pat had paid no attention to the both of us, but then the light must have hit my robe's gold brocade just so, and over Pat sauntered.

Within minutes I found myself in a makeshift Chinese fighting ring in the Heaney front hall, instructed to await the arrival of the challenger. Pat reappeared from the kitchen seconds later with Sean in tow, wearing a white terrycloth robe. Pat had found the robe and hastily drew some Chinese characters on the back for the full effect; he told us they meant "Power and Strength" but I suspect they meant "Make Tubby Puke," which, after Sean's furious roundhouse kick/sucker punch to the abdomen, I pretended to do in the bathroom between a switch-over from traditional karate to kiddie Ken-Po. Feigning illness was my only way to make it to morning, but upon hearing I'd thrown up, my dad was there. Minutes later I was back home, still in my robe, wondering what the hell had just happened. How did "Timmy's First Sleepover" suddenly turn into "Exit the Dragon and his Fancy Robe?"

I was reminded of that roundhouse kick a few months later as Sean and I ran a yard sale on the corner.

Pat wandered up, spied a few of *his* things for sale, and went into a giggling frenzy, whirling around and kicking me in the stomach. Of course, Pat had pre-approved the selection of items for sale and had even suggested a pricing strategy, but it was a lot more fun to watch me take another punch than it was to collect a few dimes for some three-wheeled matchbox cars.

It didn't end there. One of Pat's standard moves was to play the helpful and protective older brother. Out of the blue he'd suggest Sean and I play some tackle football; right then he'd produce two football helmets. The first, a professional-grade Miami Dolphins helmet, always went to Sean, and I'd get stuck with the Rams helmet, the one that had "For Decorative Purposes Only" stenciled on the back. I always suspected that the helmet came right off the Lawrence McCutcheon bobble-head doll in Sean's room, but Pat brushed my concerns aside, insisting, "You want to look real, don't you?" Pat would toss Sean his helmet, and I would watch Sean slip it on his head effortlessly. I wasn't so lucky. Pat would circle me and then pounce with all his might, grabbing my shoulders and working that helmet down on my head like trying to put a boot on a foot. My ears would take the brunt, although the chinstrap was so tight my mouth was clamped shut and I couldn't plead for help, not like there was much coming.

Retaliation was not smart. I had such a brainstorm one early evening after a particularly grueling series of throat lunges and kidney punches to my diminutive frame. My plan was to pretend I'd gone home for the night while instead I'd quietly creep to the back door where I'd throw it open and scream something to put Pat in his place. With my bicycle and the element of surprise, I couldn't fail.

I said my goodbyes and sauntered off, cradling my sore ribs as I got on my banana-seated bike, rode fifteen feet and did an abrupt U-turn. I snuck up to the door, ready to exact my revenge while the entire Heaney family sat around the dinner table. I pointed my bike on the straightest line I could find down the winding driveway and rested it on its kickstand. My plan was to yell something about Pat into the house and then hop on my bike and race down the driveway to the street and home.

With a pit in my stomach, I ripped open the door and screamed at the top of my lungs, "Pat means BRAT!" and jumped on my bike. I remember smiling like a thief who'd just stolen a loaf of stale bread for his starving family as I peddled like mad down the driveway. "I did it! I did it and I'm still alive! AIYAIYAIY HELP ME HELP ME" I yelled as I realized, all too late, that I'd forgotten about the side porch door, the door I had to pass by on my way home. Sadly, Pat did not forget this architectural fact, and upon my bold insolence, Pat calmly placed his cereal spoon down back into his crock pot of Captain Crunch, excused himself from the table and quickly walked towards the porch where he burst through the door to watch me zoom past with a reckless, uninformed grin on my face.

Sean later told me Pat's response to my revenge plot was like watching an angry cheetah take down a baby water buffalo that had wandered too far from the herd. Pat let me cruise past and then sprinted toward me. I could see his bushy hair blot out the early evening sun, his eyes burning and his fists raised. Just as I thought I might make it to the end of the driveway, Pat knocked me down with one punch to the back, my body heading east to the pavement and my bike careening west into the hedges. As I picked myself up, I saw Pat casually saunter back to the house to finish his dinner. Retaliation was a bad idea.

Most neighborhood kids, as well as Pat's parents, kept a healthy distance from the boy. The kids on the block heard my shrieks as proof, and Pat's parents had seen enough to know that Pat was not to be trifled with. I'd pray for a car horn or a scurrying squirrel to distract him, knowing that the more he hung around, the sooner he would announce the game was over and the helmet had to come off. He had no interest in the game – for him, the helmet coming on and off was the main event.

After football came boxing season. The Heaneys were big boxing fans, and they always had a few sets of gloves lying around, except that one pair was a set of tiny red gloves and the other was a pair of left-handed whoppers the size of overstuffed pillows.

Pat would relish the ring of the bell, Sean's furious footwork, and my heavy-mitted pleas for a standing eight-count and a mouth guard. My memories of those bouts are fuzzy, except that Pat always referred to me as "Little Chuckie Wepner" (a.k.a. "The Bayonne Bleeder"), and to Sean as Muhammad Ali, as in, "Work the ears, Ali! Work the ears, champ!" Sean would attack me with a ferocity that's been unmatched since. I don't know if Sean was consciously trying to knock me out or if he was working me like a speedbag with sneakers to impress Pat enough to allow us to stop. I'd like to think there were a few altruistic jabs in there, but Sean sure went at those bouts with gusto.

As Pat grew older, his love of torment shifted into a more casual mode. Instead of choreographing title fights on the front lawn, he seemed content to hang out in his attic with a few surfer buddies seeing just how high "too high" really was. Pat's love of open flames in closed spaces eventually led to a minor disaster in the Heaney house.

Banished by his mother from the kitchen for his overzealous desire for a home-cooked snack, Pat retreated into Sean's bedroom with a box of Jell-O brand pudding and a camping stove, complete with a can of sterno. Ever resourceful, Pat learned the hard way that camping stoves, semi-molten chocolate pudding and a stack of *Ranger Rick* magazines make for quite a fast-moving blaze. Needless to say, Mr. and Mrs. Heaney couldn't decide which was worse – stoking an open flame in a ten-year old's bedroom or using the fish tank to douse the out-of-control Bonfire of the Munchies before the firefighters arrived.

Eventually, I'd thought Pat had grown tired of the effort required to harass me, and through his discovery of surfing, skateboarding and herbal stress relief remedies, he drifted away, although he'd occasionally interrupt a stickball game to see if we were up for a quick two-rounder.

I thought things had finally ended when I was a sophomore in high school and Pat was home from college for vacation. He seemed genuinely happy to see me, asking me all sorts of questions about high school and the local head shops. Little did I know it was a ploy to gain my trust enough to grant him permission to cut my hair.

Lots of kids in school were getting '50's style cuts – the Stray Cats were our favorite band, and we thought the pompadour look was the in thing. So I willingly sat down on the Heaney's back porch, draped a towel around my shoulders and let Pat have at it. I should have realized something was wrong when Sean began pacing back and forth as Pat oiled up the shears, but I was ready for the *new* Pat, the college student Pat, the mature Pat who treated me like a young adult. What I was not ready for was "Pat the Psycho Stylist." In seconds, Pat took so much hair off the sides of my head that the priests at school demanded a note from my parents explaining why a nice Catholic boy with a baby face and straight A's needed a Mohawk.

I recently had the chance to reconnect with Pat at Sean's wedding. Pat was there, his orange dread-locks nicely tied in a ponytail. I hadn't seen Pat much in the last fifteen years, and I had no idea what to expect. I worked myself up into quite a spell knowing I'd see him.

The morning of the wedding, as I furtively practiced my duck-and-cover routine, Sean announced that instead of rice being thrown at the church, he and his wife-to-be, Jill, would ask the wedding guests to release Cambodian butterflies as a sign of their soaring love and commitment. Butterflies? Up close? Flying insects in our hands? I was a bowl of French Onion soup away from a complete panic attack.

Ignoring the potential for ecological disaster that foreign insects could wreak over the eastern end of Long Island, I breathed deeply and told Sean what a great idea it was! What I could sense was my scalp constricting and my stomach feeling like it was filled with the butterflies themselves. Through my fake smile I imagined Patrick chasing me down on the lawn of the church, dozens of wedding guests riveted as Pat's fists and the angry butterflies mauled me into a tuxedo-tinged pool of misery. I was a bowl of French onion soup away from having a full fear-induced seizure, but hearing that shrimp cocktail was on the menu calmed me sufficiently to help Sean box up the little critters as we headed to the chapel for the ceremony.

The wedding went off without a hitch, and I kept my distance outside the church as the guests gleefully grabbed their triangular boxes to await the signal for the insect onslaught. Having to spend time with Patrick Heaney and scores of potentially bloodthirsty winged creatures was enough for me to pass out, but by maintaining my sprinter's crouch, I kept the blood flowing to my brain.

Thankfully, Cambodian butterflies are not much for stiff spring ocean breezes because when the newlyweds gave the signal, the bugs fell to the ground and flopped around until they expired in the cold salty air. Pat stood in the midst of it, taking photos of the potential for mayhem, only to register mild disappointment as the baby Mothras failed to live up to the hype.

I spent some time with Pat at the reception. We shared some laughs even after I thanked him during my toast for teaching me "How to take a punch" his only response was, "Yeah, I guess that's true," and as we headed our separate ways, Pat placed his hand on my shoulder in what I thought was a friendly gesture, until he clamped down so hard I had to bite my lip to stop myself from yelping for help. "Take it easy, Tim," Pat muttered, as he smiled that devil smile. I think it was Pat's way of telling me that no one ever really grows up, that we are all the same people we were when we were in grade school, and that if I didn't watch it, he had two pair of boxing gloves and a football helmet in his car.

I took him at his word, stared ahead and slowly backed away. Luckily, the music, the alcohol, and the pretty colors distracted him enough for me to make a break for it into the crowd and to safety.

MY GOOD FRIEND,
DONNY BROOK

My career record as a child fighter was not stellar, but I blame the losing record on my reluctance to count the scuffle in fourth grade when I dropped the congressman's daughter with a sucker punch to the gut. In my defense, I thought she was packing heat, but it turned out to be her Bonne Bell lip smacker. If we count that one my way, I'd break even. There are two constants for every fight I've been in: first, my conviction that people are out to screw me, and second, my big mouth. The first comes from always being the shortest guy in the group, and the second comes from my desire to be as clever as possible, despite the obvious danger signs.

In high school, I averaged a fight every six months, just enough time for my face to heal and for me to forget that not everyone appreciates a snappy retort. The fights always took place over girls – either girls I was dating, had dated, or had designs on dating. You could say that in order to be a lover, I had to be a fighter, but I'd be giving myself far too much credit. I wasn't much of a fighter, and I certainly wasn't getting any loving. I was always the "step up" boyfriend for these girls, their previous or future boyfriends a few rungs down the evolutionary ladder, leaving me vulnerable to the odd assortment of aggressive Cro-Magnons looking to prove I wasn't worthy of their ladies' attention.

I had an arch-nemesis for most of my fighting years. His name was Andy, and he hated me like a village idiot hates indoor plumbing. Andy drove a Pontiac Firebird, a black one with an enormous Phoenix decal across the hood, and he wore a small golden horn around his neck favored by many of the Italian kids on Long Island. I'm not sure what the source was for Andy's hatred, but I quickly learned that he was skilled at channeling that hatred into a mean right cross, usually aimed at my freckled face.

My first experience with Andy should have been enough to convince me to leave town that night for parts unknown, but I wouldn't let him get the best of me. It all began when Andy tried, in his monosyllabic way, to explain that my old girlfriend was off-limits because his buddy had claimed her as his own. I countered with a well-measured response about how such a situation certainly didn't make Andy any tougher, and then I tossed a peppermint candy I'd been sucking at him, getting a nice chuckle from the small crowd as the sucker stuck to his cheek.

The only things I remember after that were the words, "Where's the mouth? Where's the mouth?" as Andy vaulted from behind the wheel of his car and charged me, his fists producing a mini-windstorm of pain as I tried to figure out what funny retort would stop him from beating me silly. I decided to take the initiative and throw the first punch, which only made him angrier. It's a bad sign of what's to come when your opponent stifles a laugh as your meek fist glances off his Italian marble chin. When Andy was finished, I had two black eyes, a fat lip, a chipped front tooth, and a sprained collarbone, not bad for twenty seconds of work. He also walloped my buddy in the chest and then decked my new girlfriend down to the ground before returning his attention to me for one more kick to the neck.

The next morning, I made my way to the breakfast table, hiding inside my hooded sweatshirt until my mother saw my face and demanded an explanation. I fessed up at once, even providing Andy's home address, vital signs and brand of mouthwash (Lavoris). My mom picked up the phone immediately and started dialing Andy's house, but my dad convinced her not to call, knowing that I'd probably had it coming. I've always wondered what the breakfast scene looked like at Andy's house that morning – most likely a family of cave dwellers trying to coax a flame out of a pile of wet leaves in the family room as they drew scenes of Andy's victory in charcoal on the walls.

A few months later, I ran into Andy again, having successfully avoided him at every turn until then. This time, he stated clearly that he was looking to fight me. "You wanna fight?" he asked, although I thought the question rather rhetorical. To give myself time to spot the best place to hide, I tried distracting him, asking, "A donnybrook, you say? A scrape, a row, a healthy round of fisticuffs?" prompting him to note, "I don't know who the fuck Donny Brook is but you're gettin' a mouthful a Chicklets, pork chop!" Actually, I got a mouthful of Timberland that night, although anyone who saw the fight swore I stung him hard before getting karate-kicked in my head until Andy's glutes got sore.

Once Andy had moved on to bigger and better targets, I had to contend with his henchmen for a few years. Once I got jumped by one of Andy's troglodytes, Glen, for joking a bit too loud to a friend about Glen's work-release program giving him a weekend pass. He gave me quite a stomping, and it would have been worse until I convinced him that I'd just seen Twisted Sister at the ice cream store, and if he hurried, maybe he could share Dee Snyder's Matterhorn with him. Glen was always a sucker for free ice cream.

When I got to college, I was ready to establish my fighting credentials, but I was quickly informed that fighting was grounds for immediate expulsion. Fearing a lifetime of weekly bouts with Andy and his clan of cave bears back home on Long Island, I kept my mouth shut and hit the books, leaving the fighting for the summers.

I spent most of my summers as a camp counselor, and we were always targets for the locals, each of them waiting in line to "teach them college shits" a lesson or two. My summertime exploits often amounted to uttering a few pithy maxims while the locals surrounded me like jackals. I'd then try to hold my own until my friends rescued me. "Holding my own" meant running the serpentine while shrieking for help, but it served its purpose, and we won most of the fights. A man has to know his limitations, and always being the smallest guy in the ring forced me to be creative.

But what's a fighter to do once college is over, camp counseling is done, and a harmless punch or two can get you eight to ten for assault and battery? I argue there's always a need to settle things the old fashioned way. I finally got my college friends involved during a weekend down south. We were hitting it big in a casino (I was up $18), and fresh from another winning hand, we made our way to the slots. I dropped a chip and watched it roll right underneath a blackjack table. I went to retrieve it, and as I picked it up, a well-scrubbed fellow in an argyle sweater vest appeared above me, grabbing me by the collar and demanding I return his buddy's chip to the table.

I explained he had the wrong guy, that I was picking up what was mine. That's when that little voice inside my head began screaming, "He's trying to get one over on you! Quick, say something and make a dash for the Pit Boss!" So I made a comment about his snappy sweater vest and something about tickets for the poetry lecture, which didn't sit too well. As he dragged me towards his table and his similarly groomed playmates, I yelled for my buddies, who came to my defense. I situated myself behind the largest friend in our group and then expressed how I really felt about being called a thief by Fred MacMurray's long-lost brother.

My pugilistic poetry-professor opponent didn't like what I had to say, and he tried to take a swing at me, but the six Midori Sours had rendered his left jab somewhat lacking. His friends stopped him and off we went into the night, chalking another **W** in the win column for me.

Since high school, I'd convinced myself that I'd ended up getting the best of Andy, that I'd made something of my life, had a beautiful family, a college degree, and a good job, but I'm not so sure anymore.

A few years ago, my wife and I went home to my parents' house with our newborn son. The doorbell rang, and I hopped up to get it, expecting the pizza delivery boy. I opened the door and just about loosed my bowels on the welcome mat. There, with a hot pizza in his hands, stood Andy himself. He didn't seem surprised at all to see me as he slouched there with an uneven grin on his face, his Firebird idling in the driveway. My first thought was how embarrassing it would be to get my ass kicked in front of my infant son, and then I started scanning the memory banks for the meanest zinger I could muster, something like, "Sorry, the Gorilla Cage is full. Try the zoo down the street," or "Here's a tip: don't play with matches!" as I'd slam the door in his face. Instead, I just took the pizza, handed Andy the money, thanked him, and closed the door, realizing I'd overtipped him in the process. We said nothing to each other more than that, and he must have been laughing to himself as he dragged his knuckles down the path to his car.

We sat down to eat our pizza, our baby son sleeping peacefully in my wife's arms, and I couldn't help but thinking I'd really blown my chance for ultimate victory. What a golden opportunity to finally stick it to the guy who'd run me scared for years, but I didn't have it in me. That little voice inside me has grown more intent on enjoying a nice hot meal and my family's company than screaming about the size of the chip on my shoulder. Besides, people tell me my son's going to be pretty big, and with him behind me, I bet I'll have a winning record in no time.

WILLY WONKA AND THE LAMENT
OF THE LITTLE MAN

It's not easy being a little man in a big man's world. The world I live in was made for someone taller because it seems I'm always a footstool away from acceptance. I'm that man who's stuck in the in-between land of being just tall enough not to be considered really short and a bit too short to be just plain average, the one who won't ask for a booster seat at the barbershop as his feet dangle above the floor. Only occasionally do I hear things like, "Mommy, why does that chubby little boy have a mustache?" or "Hey, check out the fat kid drinking a Whiskey Sour!"

I was always small for my age, but I never gave it much thought. I probably should have known something was amiss when I went to the circus and begged my dad for a poster of Mishu, the little Russian impresario, instead of Lars the Lion Tamer, like all the other kids. Mishu topped out at thirty-three inches, but he had a heart twice the size, or at least that's what I told myself. Coincidentally, I think that's what killed the little fella – his heart was too big and his tiny limbs and muscles couldn't keep up. No child should look up to a man who dresses in Oshkosh bib overalls, but there I was in the front row, frantically waving my souvenir flashlight at the slightest glimpse of the tiny Slavic superstar.

Also, my nickname at summer camp was, "Midgie." I thought it was a Native American word meaning "Swims like an otter," but I came to learn it was closer to "He who wears bells on his sneakers." The nickname grew crueler each summer as the puberty fates handed out height to the other kids while I patiently waited for inches that never came.

When I was finally old enough to drink in bars, I quickly realized bartenders favor tall guys. Even today I could stand at the bar, on my tippy-toes, wearing a tuxedo and top hat, waving a $100 bill in the air, and the 6'3" homeless guy with a single black tooth and a handful of Monopoly money would get his beer before me.

I've been tempted to start shopping at the Husky Boys section at the mall, but I can't bear the thought of buying clothes meant for a beefy twelve-year old. Try to find pants off the rack for a guy with a 36" waist and a 28" inseam. It's next to impossible. It's always humiliating asking the sales person if her store carries them. I usually get a quick, "Um, nope. Check the website," just before she darts to the back room, cackling to her co-workers about the sawed-off runt looking for a Dapper Dan outfit.

Finding shoes is just as tough. My wife has a bunch of nephews, all truly Brobdingnagian, who always seem to be wearing new sneakers. During one visit, I had a great idea. These kids must have a few pair lying around in my size, so I asked the oldest one, Robbie, if he had any size-seven sneakers. Robbie, who was thirteen at the time, gave me one of those looks that said, "I crap things bigger than you." Such a look wasn't much help, so I asked his brother, Paul. Paul was a twelve-year-old budding basketball star, and I figured if anyone had an extra size-seven, Paul would be the guy. Granted, they might come from his box of baby mementos, but I have no problem with wearable heirlooms. He told me he couldn't ever remember having such small feet and figured he jumped from size five to size nine overnight, something that probably happens all the time in the land of giants.

I had size-seven feet at age fourteen and my feet haven't grown a whisker since. Around my fifteenth birthday, I bought a pair of size-eight winter boots, sure I would grow into them. I threw them out a few years ago, sick of schlepping around in boots too big for me.

When I was a kid, a sneaker store in our town used to have NBA Hall of Famer Bob Lanier's basketball sneaker on display in a glass case. The shoe was a white, three-striped leather Adidas the size of my upper torso, and I'd gaze longingly at it every chance I got, wondering if, in a water-related emergency, I could use it as a canoe and paddle to safety.

I fight the short man's battle every day, and life as a husband and father provides no respite from the world of the big. My wife, half a foot taller, loves to use the top of the refrigerator to store our kids' lunch boxes. Every morning I strain my hamstrings trying to leap up and snag them as I make the day's meals. My son sits, impassive, watching me jump about like a point guard for the Washington Generals defending Meadowlark Lemon. There are items on the upper shelves in closets that I've never seen, presumably advice books for women who marry short men. And that shelf picker I keep hinting at for Father's Day gets ignored every year.

My wife doesn't do any of this on purpose, and she is sensitive to being married to someone a tad smaller. She rarely wears heels, tends to run from a camera whenever we're next to each other, and when she can't run, she usually bends down to make sure her head is included in the shot, like a teacher in a fourth-grade field trip photo. I must be one of the few husbands around who has to set ground rules when he plays a friendly game of H-O-R-S-E with his wife. No taunting, no elbows and no dunking! She usually gives me the outside jumper, but the key is all hers.

But the greatest reminders for me about my stature are my kids. My son will soon be my height, and he continues to grow at record pace. When he was younger, he got upset at the idea that he'd be taller than his dad, but lately, he's been eyeballing me, probably wondering how fast he could pin me for my wallet. In a few years, he'll be bigger than me – already his hands are like fleshy oven mitts, while mine are more like Cabbage Patch doll hands. I fear a complete loss of authority once he's taller.

Any parent, no matter what, wins some respect right out of the gate in the delivery room, but when you remain the same size and the child continues to grow, the entire parental authority structure gives way and we're left with anarchy. Thank God my wife is tall – I can count on her to keep him in line.

The most evident example of my son's secret shame at having a wee man as a father came last summer. We watched *Willy Wonka and the Chocolate Factory* before he headed to bed. As I tucked him in, my son turned to me and asked about the movie, wondering how they made it. I explained that it wasn't real, that they used actors, that Augustus Gloop probably didn't do his own stunts. But my son was undeterred. "But what about those orange men? Those oompah loompah little guys? How did they get them so short?"

"Well," I said, doing my best to figure out the difference between a dwarf and a midget, "there are some people who are just naturally shorter than the rest of us (using the word "us" seemed to be the right move at the time). "They're called midgets, and they're born that way." My son froze, stared at me, and swallowed, seeming to choose his words very carefully. In that split-second, I knew I'd stumbled into the wrong conversation and wanted to disappear, knowing what he was about to say. Before I could distract him, he asked it.

"So are *you* a midget?" he asked, plain and simple. And he sat there, waiting for a response. So, like any short dad would do, I got defensive.

"Did you just call me a midget?" I said.

"No!" he replied. "I just *asked* if you were a midget! I never *called* you a midget!" he exclaimed.

"It's the same thing!" I yelled. "Why do you think I'm a midget? Because I'm shorter than all the other dads?"

"I never called you a midget, but, yeah, come to think of it, you are the tiniest dad at the bus stop," he added. I was tempted to continue the conversation and defend my 5'5" statue for all its non-midgetness, but I backed off. He's up to my shoulder already, and his hand could palm my noggin like a ripe Cassava melon. And I didn't want to dredge up the still-painful memory of the "Mr. Small Peeps" remark he'd made a while back, a comment I refuse to dignify with an explanation. A mini-man has to pick his battles, and larger ones loom, no doubt.

So I endure - a bitty man beating back against the current of a bigger world. But I am optimistic. I'm pretty sure I could beat my daughter in H-O-R-S-E, and I won't even need to dunk, at least not for a few years.

DANCING FOOL

I like to dance, and I'm not talking about the fancy stuff, like waltzing or ballroom dancing. I'm talking about the let-loose, get-sweaty, pull-the-hamstring kind of dancing, and I can't get enough of it. Being a bit on the hefty side my entire life does give me reason to hesitate before hitting the floor, what with the potential for my man-breasts to bounce wildly, but I can't help it. I need to get jiggly with it as often as possible.

My desire to shake what God gave me hasn't always been easy. During gym class in sixth grade, my free-form stylings to the comforting beats of the "Alley Cat" got me noticed by Mr. Wagner, the music teacher. He demanded I join him in bringing "Disco Galaxy" to life – his vision for the Stewart School Spring Concert, telling me the climax, a five-song Bee Gees medley, would give me a chance "to show everyone what a great dancer" I was. Flattery worked and before I knew it, I was getting measured for my costume (form-fitting black turtleneck, white flare pants, and rainbow suspenders a la Mork from Ork) between rehearsals with my backup dancers, who went by the name "Violet Delight."

We practiced for months, working on my swim move, when to drop to my knees, and when to twirl Delight while Violet pranced in the background. We'd practice over lunch, and to this day, the sight of a Carnation breakfast bar makes me break into a nervous sweat. I ate them to lose weight, fearing that the unsightly image of a disco stud with pre-teen rolls of pudge yearning to break free from the tight turtleneck might be too much for the K through 6 audience to handle.

I kept this news secret from family and friends, my brother's chants of "Death to Disco" ringing in my ears. Besides, I knew my family had no dancing ability; other than my mom's elbow chicken dance routine, I'd never seen any O'Shea dancing, running, or even walking quickly, for that matter. And as much as the thought of disco dancing in front of 500 kids and parents was terrifying, I liked the idea that people would see me work my soul magic and the moves I could pump out.

Things went horribly wrong the day before opening night, just before Disco Galaxy's big bang. At dress rehearsal, Mrs. Gatley, our art teacher, grabbed me and exclaimed, "There's just one thing missing from this show. Face Paint!" My heart sank as Mrs. Gatley explained that she and Mr. Wagner had decided to "add some excitement" to the show by dolling me up like "one of those makeup rock and rollers." I knew where this would end up as images of Gene Simmons and Ace Frehley filled my mind.

Seconds later, my face was covered with a Kiss-inspired dragon scale/star combo design. I'd been conscripted into the Kiss Army Disco Division, and I was not happy. Friends had already begun to figure out what I was up to, and Delight sure couldn't keep any secrets, but *this*, this was *much* worse. Not only was I dressed like an overweight apprentice mime, but now I was covered in Max Factor greasepaint, forced to combine the sexy, pinpoint moves of the Hustle with the drug-induced look of a mysterious glam rocker. I was a dancing contradiction.

The next morning I feigned illness, trying to convince my mother I was sick and getting worse by the minute, blaming both the bossanova *and* the face paint, but no luck. All she said was, "Hurry up or you'll miss the bus. There will be hundreds of people out there tonight waiting to see my little dumpling jump around to disco music." As I ran out the door, I thought I heard her mumble, "And I won't be one of them, you disco dork," but I could have been mistaken.

That night, I sat slumped backstage, my black turtleneck tight against my flabby midsection, slight pimples surfacing under the half-inch smear of black-and-white face paint, watching Violet Delight practice their moves in earnest concentration. I said to myself, "If this is my fifteen minutes of fame, my life is gonna suck!" But I figured if my life was headed downhill, at least I could go down nimbly. I whispered a short prayer, threw down my cup of Strawberry Yoo-Hoo, went out there and nailed the routine.

I don't remember much except the oboe-driven transition of "Night Fever" into "More Than a Woman" just before the curtain fell to thunderous applause. Someone from my family must have been there because I have an action photo from the event. I stand center-stage giving the Tony Manero Arm Stab to the Sky, my undulating belly and ill-fitting trousers making quite a scene as Violet Delight whirl in the background. That night I accepted my dancing ability, not as a burden, but as a gift for all those who had the stomach to watch.

And the dancing would continue. In high school I danced all the time at parties; my friend Sean and I had a routine on the dance floor of any keg party or basement beer ball bash. I'd flop to the floor, motionless, and he'd stand over me and grab my temples, shocking me back to life. It was our signature move and always got big applause.

We never hit the dance floor with girls in mind. We were there to tear it up solo or as a duo, the standing rule being that if we heard a song that had motion, beat, and energy, we had an obligation to get on the floor and dance like we had hot coals in our slacks.

Once at a Friday night mixer at my Catholic high school, I danced into such a frenzy that the brothers confronted me, insisting that I was high on "the drugs" for moving with such abandon. It was tough convincing these male nuns I was only high on Elvis Costello and Joe Jackson music, but that's what a celibate life will get you – an innate inability to connect the opening bars of "Look Sharp" with a vigorous shake of the rump.

A few years ago I went to New Orleans for Jazz Fest, and it took me and my buddy Erik about three hours on Bourbon Street (aided by generous and inexpensive servings of alcohol) to find our happy move groove. We started dancing in a bar, one that opened out onto the street. As the songs got better, our dancing got more intense, the kegs kept flowing, and we kept shuckin' and jivin'. Pretty soon a small crowd gathered to cheer us on, prompting a third friend to put a cup on the ground for pocket change. Within five minutes we'd earned around $20. Yes, the journey from grade school disco dancing in sexually ambiguous face paint to shaking it for beer money thousands of miles away from home is something to be proud of, and I don't want it to end.

I fear, though, that my chance for dance may be evaporating. It's wrong and immature, but I still base the success of a party on how much dancing took place. I haven't been to a marginally successful party in a long time. A few neighbors and I tried to plan a dance party, but the idea never took off. I wanted kegs of beer, a professional DJ, and a huge dance floor, but they were thinking instead of a few warm wine-cooler four-packs, a half-dozen Kool and the Gang songs taped off the radio, and moving the ottoman into the corner.

I dance to be seen, to make the scene, and your living room, although cozy and nicely appointed, is not the place to break out the Pencil Sharpener or the Dry Hump, the Fish Hop or the Donkey Kong, the Clam Digger or the Angel Dust Stomp. With some luck, my dancing gene may live on in my children. Before he hit kindergarten, my son had a top-notch "Riverdance" routine. Sam would beg us to turn off the lights, turn up the music, and whip the flashlight back and forth as he, shirtless and ecstatic, danced himself into an Irish-American spectacle of joyful movement. He was lost in the moment, just like I tend to get, and I saw visions of dance floor success in his future. My daughter also gives me reason to hope. Her weekly dance lessons, coupled with her father's tutoring, have given Maisie some *serious* moves. I do worry that her talents will lead to a future littered with dollar bills and sequined outfits, but for now, I'm thrilled that she shakes her bon bon at the mere hint of a beat.

And this need to dance never really goes away. Just a few weekends ago, I did some of my best dancing at my friend Jay's wedding in Virginia. Whether it was the vodka, the ear-splitting notes of Santana's "Smooth," or the sight of the groom's inebriated and intimidating older sister's demands that I dance with her, I can't say. But I do remember working my body into a sweat-drenched lather, kicking out the jams as the bride's elderly Vietnamese relatives watched in shocked horror. Their distaste didn't matter one bit – when the Running Man's mojo is upon you, you have no choice but to keep sprinting to the beat. International relations be damned! Granted, I had to ice my lower back for a few days as penance, but it was worth every strained lumbar. Dancers like me handle pain with grace (and Advil, *plenty* of Advil).   So armed with enough medicine, two talented kids, and a good rhythm, I expect to be a dancing fool for years to come. But the face paint and suspenders stay at home.

DESTINY FOR A DOLLAR

brother Mike believes in destiny. He thinks that fate has already chosen his life's course, a path he's powerless to alter in any meaningful way. Mike's destiny, he explained, is "To win the lottery so I never have to work a day in my life again." He said this just hours after coming within a single digit of being America's newest multi-millionaire, courtesy of the New York State Lottery Commission.

Mike was one number away from hitting it big - $15 million big. Imagine what $15 million would do for you. Quite a bit, I'm sure. He was so close to having his six computer-generated, randomly-selected lottery numbers match those on the six ping-pong balls jumbled around in a huge hopper and forced up by hot air - and, Mike supposes, the hand of fate. Painfully, five numbers matched, but the sixth didn't; Mike needed a "26" and got a "25" instead. One measly digit separated him from fulfilling his destiny, which is not too bad for a guy who hasn't reached thirty yet.

He had noble ideas for how to spend his winnings: pay off all debts for his parents, brothers and sisters, plan a huge family vacation to Bermuda, and "tell my boss that my relationship with this company just isn't working out, take the subway to a bar, and get totally wasted for the rest of the day." Now that's a plan from a guy who doesn't need one. With destiny calling the shots, all Mike needs to do is to keep playing the lottery. Even fate needs a dollar and a dream.

As a kid, I remember reading a story in *Ripley's Believe it or Not* about a woman dropping her wedding ring down the sink only to discover it in the belly of a fish she was preparing for dinner at the same sink months later. My mind swelled with the sequence of events that put the ring back on the woman's finger. So many "what if's" pop up to make you crazy. Was that fate? Did destiny return the ring or was it just a staggering set of circumstances? Did the halibut think it was his destiny to find what looked like the coolest thing he'd ever swallowed, only to end up on a dinner plate, served with shallots and a light cream sauce? Or was he just near the wrong drain pipe at the wrong time?

I envy Mike for subscribing to the idea that fate has a hand in his future on Easy Street. I envy him for believing, for *knowing* that his numbers will hit someday, and that every miserable morning at work will soon be a distant memory for him as he eats bowls of Ambrosia salad wearing nothing but his bathrobe and fancy slippers. And Mike's lucky to be alive now. In another time, Mike's dual love of gambling and predetermination would have branded him a warlock and gotten himself pressed between two giant millstones until he gave up his devilish ways. But today, he can go on buying lottery tickets whenever and wherever he wants, convinced that fate is only a dollar away.

I have no faith in fate, for fish or family. I think we are surrounded by circumstances and random events that sometimes converge at the right time but usually don't. Our lots in life have nothing to do with the unseen hand of fate. Destiny is nothing more than a conviction that our lives are tough enough that there's got to be a greater plan than this. I would have made a lousy Calvinist, I realize, but I just don't see my life that way. Life's what you make of what you have around you and inside you.

Mike's tiny taste of destiny did pocket him $2,200, but he has his sights set higher. I'm convinced he has a better chance of training a squirrel to change his car's oil than he does of hitting all six numbers, especially after getting so close and not winning, but he's undeterred.

Instead, this near-brush with indiscriminate wealth has emboldened him. "I'll be more aggressive from now on," he told me. I wish him all the best, but I think he'll be working for a while, the silver remnants of the day's scratch-off tickets staining his fingers as he wanders off to the lucky bodega, the one "where I almost won the Pick Four that time I was wearing my winner socks." I don't have the heart to tell him there is no such thing as destiny. Destiny's a sucker's bet, just like the lottery. I will admit, though, that I've got my holiday plans on hold. Christmas in Bermuda would be kind of nice.

WILL WORK FOR LOVE

There are few jobs in this world I can see really loving, although I wouldn't know because I've never had one that qualifies. I've had some fun jobs, some challenging jobs, and one or two easy jobs, but I've yet to find that job that makes me declare, "This is the best job in the world, and I would be miserable without it." This is not to say I don't value work as a way to pay my bills, because I do; but I won't ever trust those people who smile and say, "I love my job!"

What's there to love? Can you really love delivering mail door to door in all sorts of weather? Think of the shoes you'd go through. Should I believe you when you tell me that shoveling bat guano in the zoo is your life's dream? Or selling life insurance, refilling ATMs, grilling burgers, or painting fences? Most of us are still trying to figure out what the hell happened from high school to now, and why didn't I send in the drawing of that turtle to that art school? Damn, I could be a cartoonist right now! So we end up taking a job that pays us as much as we can get, while our dream job is always something we read about in the magazines with the ad in the back about drawing that turtle to get into art school.

I have a friend who once told me the whole reason he works is to earn money to buy things to improve himself so he appears attractive to women. He'd boiled it down to a simple equation: "I work for money to buy clothes and running sneakers and a leather couch and hair gel so that women will want to have sex with me." I've always admired his ability to cut through the BS, but then he went off and slaved for years as a waiter in New York until his break came as an actor. He may have claimed to work to have more sex, but he ended up finding the passion to stick with his job enough to be satisfied, maybe even to love it. I've yet to have such luck.

The first job I had was as an eight-year-old salesman hawking eggplant, zinnia, and wax bean seeds door-to-door. If I'd been on the Tycoon Career Path, I'd now brag about parlaying that $18.43 into a nation-wide franchise of coin-operated laundries or gasket factories, but I invested the profits in a pack of candy smokes and a fistful of Charleston Chews. Nice to know that when my ship came in, I was too busy picking nougat out of my teeth to notice.

In my pre-teen years, my parents forced me to find employment, my older brother setting such a keen example of hard work in low-paying jobs that I had no choice. Danny had been an all-star paperboy for years, perfecting the art of balancing stacks of Sunday newspapers on his knee while hustling down the street on his ten-speed. When Danny graduated from the daily paper to the women's department at Saks 5th Avenue, my parents decided the route was too lucrative to relinquish, and I got the job. I hadn't really applied for it, but I accepted my fate and awaited my first visit from the boss, who'd show me the ropes.

My brother had already become too engrossed in his new job at Saks to afford me any advice, so engrossed that a few weeks into the job, Danny found himself locked in the fur vault after closing. I heard a rumor that when the security guards found him, he was wearing a floor-length white mink overcoat and a bright pink fedora, slapping the mannequins around, mumbling something about "Late payments from my ladies." We could never prove it, and Danny was silent on the matter.

My life as a paperboy lasted eight minutes. The boss came to the house to drop off the circulars, explaining that even though it was Thursday, these were for Sunday's delivery. I quickly deduced two things paramount to my potential failure as a paperboy: first, no one told me that we delivered four-day old news to our customers, and second, I had an irrational fear of paper cuts. I watched the boss walk down the front steps, counted to ten, and announced to no one in particular, "I quit." My parents were too despondent over their first-born's newfound love of ermine stoles to notice, and I escaped, unscathed and unemployed for a while.

As a teenager, I considered working at McDonalds, reading somewhere that one in five Americans work at the Golden Arches at some point. Never one to ignore my duty as an American, I researched it a bit and determined that McDonalds' recruiting slogan, "Friends, Fun and Flexible Hours," smelled too much like loving your job, and there was no need to start down that path. Besides, my sister Molly had worked there for a while, and she didn't seem to have any more friends or fun from it, although she did get to keep her snappy blue-and-white-striped uniform, a staple in her Halloween repertoire for years to come.

With my fast-food jones behind me, I took a job at the local supermarket. This was a place I'd spent many mornings with my mom over the years, and she was friendly with all the employees. My application was fast-tracked, and within days, I found myself bagging groceries in my red vest and my oversized "Ask me, I'm here to help" button on my lapel. It took a few weeks to determine the source of the friendliness among the workers. I wandered down into the break room and interrupted what could have passed for a party on the "Rasta Man Vibration" tour bus, except that Bob Marley was really Kenny the Hawaiian produce guy, and Peter Tosh was really Dave the Deli guy. As I peered through the haze, I realized most of the guys I'd been saying "Hi" to for years were also saying "Hi," but only in the context of, "I am so high right now, and that chubby kid with the freckles keeps bugging me about where the Goober Grape is at."

After being the hard-working, drug-free employee for a few months, I finally succumbed to the pressure, Andrew in the deli convincing me that "A six-hour shift seems like forty-five minutes when you're stoned." I also figured that the cockroach races in the basement would be more exciting. Those six hours felt more like two days after sharing a joint with my co-workers, especially when I realized I'd marked around two hundred rolls of toilet paper with a $37 price tag and had to unpeel each sticker and retag them all, Mr. Pintabona, the store manager, standing behind me the entire time. And the cockroach derby was like my own little horror movie, convincing me that recreational drugs and semi-skilled labor weren't a good combo for me.

I lasted six months before quitting to go skiing for a week in Canada. Okay, technically I was fired, but I tried to tell Mr. Pintabona that I quit as he screamed at me over the phone in between bites of his mortadella sub.

That was the only job where I was fired outright, although I was laid off a few years back. I should have seen that one coming. I was really starting to like it and was getting paid far more than I should have been. When word spread around the office that day, I had three or four hours to contemplate my fate. The minutes ticked by as, one by one, my co-workers answered their phones, sulked off to a conference room, and emerged ten minutes later with looks of embarrassment and dismay on their faces.

I felt like a sailor on the *USS Indianapolis* sunk by a Japanese torpedo, watching my fellow sailors get plucked down by the sharks as I waited to feel the jaws clamp around my own feet. A friend came by to assure me that, "If they haven't called by now, you're all set! It's almost noon. You made it!" Just as I reached for a high-five, my phone rang, prompting my friend to say, "Oops. Spoke too soon. Later!" as he evaporated into the misty gloom. As I made the walk of shame back to my desk, I reminded myself that I got what I deserved, too close to loving my job.

None of my jobs has sparked my imagination enough to make me love it. Just recently, I attended a conference for work and sat next to a guy who told me he "was in transition." What he was trying to say was he got laid off from his last job and was now, like me, attending boring conferences, looking for answers in the dim lighting and stale pastries.

And that's when it hit me – that's what my problem is – I have a job, but I always feel like I'm in transition too. I haven't yet found the job that's made me want to stick around long enough to consider myself a company man, and I don't think I really ever want to. I fear feeling like I've finally arrived, that I don't need to keep moving. It's like Bob Dylan once sang: "Those not busy being born are busy dying." For me, that translates into "Those not busy wondering what working somewhere else is like are busy being boring."

So when people remind me that the goal is to find a job I love, I wish I could agree; but for me, I won't ever find it, so I enjoy the transitions. Perhaps admitting that I've held twelve jobs in the thirteen years since I graduated from college should be a bad thing, but who cares? Right now I love the fact that I've got a sharpened pencil, some blank white paper, and a pretty good drawing of a turtle in front of me. Maybe this time I'll drop it in the mail.

NATIONAL TV DAY

If you'd been listening to the radio on the night of September 26, 1960, you would have sworn that Richard Nixon would be the next President of the United States. It's been said that citizens turned their radios off after the debate and dreamt of a newly-elected President Nixon frolicking in the Florida surf in his navy blue suit and wingtips. Radio listeners were sure Nixon had debated that pumpkin-headed rich kid from Boston into submission, only to wake up the next day and realize their man had lost. The 70 million people who watched the television broadcast had a different experience. To them, Richard Nixon looked like he'd shaved with the dull end of a butter knife.

John F. Kennedy was perfect for TV - his tan skin and boyish good looks distracted the viewers enough that they didn't bother listening to what he had to say. People liked what they saw, and Kennedy became President six weeks later.

Nixon eventually realized it would be foolish to ignore the power of television. And if he were alive today, he'd marvel at how America's grown to embrace it. We watch lots of television. We watch it at home, in the gym, in our hospital beds, on airplanes, in the back of taxi cabs, and in bars. We can order our TV with rabbit ears, in UHF or VHF, digitally, via satellite or in high-definition. We can buy TVs that fit in the palms of our hands, TVs with screens inside of screens, and plasma TVs so big they take up entire walls in our houses. We can catch a minister railing against the sins of the flesh on one channel and witness those same sins in action just one click away. We can watch a live baseball game, pause it to refill the bowl of Funyuns, and return without missing a single strike! Is this a great country or what! And, like any proud American, I spend plenty of time with my TV – enough time to realize that something must be done to recognize the importance of television in my life and in the lives of all citizens.

This is why I now propose we set aside a day on our nation's calendar dedicated to the great American institution of television. I even have the perfect day – September 26 - commemorating that night in 1960 when Richard Nixon realized that a good argument and a firmly held position are no match for perfect hair and a great shave. Most of our holidays remind of us of our fallen heroes, like Pocahontas on Thanksgiving or Johnny Appleseed on Arbor Day, and September 26, National TV Day, would remind us that some gave all, or at least their immediate political future, so the rest of us can watch TV all day, every day - anywhere and everywhere we choose.

We'd celebrate National TV Day by staying indoors in our pajamas, comfortably taking in a steady stream of "Mr. Belvedere" and "American Gladiator" reruns, pocket fisherman and bamboo steamer infomercials, live-feed simulcasts, made-for-TV movies, tape-delayed sporting events, and lots of dramatizations of the Nixon-Kennedy debates, but this time, we'd have an interactive chat scrolling on the bottom of the screen: "Forget Formosa! JFK's the dreamiest!" We'd televise town meetings to argue about whether Joanie really did love Chachi and hold scholarly roundtables, debating the cultural significance of such phrases as "Kid Dynomite!" and "Sock it to me!" Dr. Phil could do a two-hour show on bookwork kids and the lousy parents who are to blame: "It don't take a polecat eatin' a sweet potato to see that your kids need more TV, dagnubit!" Frankly, I get dizzy with the possibilities such a holiday holds.

I must admit the desire for this holiday is somewhat personal. As a kid, I did my best to make *every* day National TV day. It worked for a few years, until I kept bringing home failing grades on such essays as "Ponch and Jon – Way Cooler than Lewis and Clarke," and "Jabber Jaw - The James K. Polk of Cartoon Sharks!" My mother was convinced I was developing an incurable addiction to television, and after one more off-handed comment from me about her being "no Carol Brady," my mom took drastic action, purchasing a set of tiny TV locks that fit over the plugs. She ignored the fact that an addict will resort to anything to get his fix, and I broke those locks in seconds with a paper clip and wad of Bubble Yum. But she'd made her point, and I still carry some of that guilt with me. But through the adoption of National TV Day, I can find at least one day a year to do nothing but bask in the glow of the reassuring warmth of the TV, knowing that my fellow citizens are doing the same exact thing, casting off the shame of too much TV once and for all.

True, National TV Day won't be for everyone at first. For example, my older brother and his wife will recoil at the suggestion that TV gets its own day, over National Hug a Soy Farmer Day or National Read a Book with No Pictures Day, let's say. They don't watch *any* TV, but during a visit to my house a few years ago, they watched more TV in that one weekend than they had for the past fifteen years. At one point I suggested they get some sleep, but the two of them just sat there, puddles of drool forming in their laps as they watched a subtitled documentary about the gestation habits of the Peruvian tree sloth. They realized that a life without TV is a life not worth living, and I am sure National TV Day would quickly become their most sacred day.

Finally, I do recognize the stiff resistance this holiday will get from the other well-established holidays, each claiming its exclusive hold on television-centric celebration. Thanksgiving will try its patented Underdog float attack, and I expect Christmas will come swinging a fistful of Zuzu's petals, but National TV Day will endure. The only holiday that has any real chance against this idea is New Year's Day, which, as far as I can tell, only exists so we can watch the Olestra Toilet Bowl, live from Akron, Ohio. But in the end, New Year's Day, like Thanksgiving, Christmas, Halloween and the rest, will bow down to the power that is television in America.

So let's give it a whirl this September 26. Call in sick to work, cancel the kids' harpsichord lessons, and pay your respects to the one thing in America that unites us all.

And when National TV Day comes to pass, somewhere the ghosts of John F. Kennedy and Richard Nixon will smile, happy that the rest of us finally get the joke.

THE PANIC OF OPENING DAY

Some may call April the cruelest month for poetic reasons, but I see it another way. April's cruel all right, and it's pretty simple. Baseball season is here, and everything's coming apart. I can already predict how it will be. First, I'm caught reading the box scores alone in my room in May; then, in mid-July, I'll get busted chugging a can of Red Bull to stay awake for the West Coast broadcasts; finally, in late October, they'll find me hiding in the linen closet, smearing voodoo paste on my torso, mumbling something about my dreams of a World Series victory zipping past me like a called third strike. But not this year. No way. This is the year I get my priorities in order, the year my family comes first, the year I start caring less about Pedro Martinez's hair gel and more about my physical and emotional well-being.

First, above all, I won't try to explain how one can be a loyal Mets fan and a rabid Red Sox fan at the same time, except that it's kind of like being a Jew for Jesus. Next, I will stop believing I can control a game's events from my couch; this mental ability of mine peaked during the 1986 World Series, and it's been downhill ever since. In addition, I will not question Red Sox right fielder Trot Nixon's claim that God gave him the strength to hit a homerun to beat the A's in the 2003 playoffs, even though the Holy Spirit seems to have been on a smoking break when Trot couldn't catch a fly ball in deep right field at Yankee Stadium in Game 7 of the pennant.

There are plenty of other things I commit to changing about my life this season. For example, I will not get liquored up on Peach Schnapps and hop the railing with my son to attack the first base coach of the Kansas City Royals on May 8th at Fenway Park, unless provoked unnecessarily. Also, when the Yankees are in town, I will not yell things at Derek Jeter, such as, "Hey Jeter, I saw the matriarch of your brood in a local establishment this morning, and she was quite inebriated!"

Similarly, I will not be goaded into foolish bets with my friends from Philadelphia, neither for the games their team plays at Fenway Park this summer nor for the Phillies' chances against the Mets this season, however slight they may be. Besides, the image of my buddy Chickenhead in a leopard-skin athletic supporter is reason enough not to wager.

In addition, I will not try to calculate how many David Ortizes, stacked on top of each other, it would take to reach the Monster Seats if one were to use a Stacked Big Papi ladder to reach them. While at Fenway Park, I will not justify cutting the line for one more beer before they shut the taps off in the 7th inning like that time a few years ago. Although that lady was drunk, her crutches were not defective, and I did not slip on an Italian ice as I then claimed.

Before any playoff appearance by the Red Sox or Mets, I will not rub the nose of the Mo Vaughn Bobblehead doll that sits in a protective case on my dresser in a crude attempt at anti-Red Sox and Mets reverse mojo. And I will resist the urge to take anxiety-relieving prescription drugs just before the start of a big game, much like I did before both Game 7's against the A's and Yankees, unless, of course, I am alone in the house and we're out of Peach Schnapps.

To be a better father and husband, I will not purchase Direct TV's MLB Extra Innings package to watch some of the sixty games that are broadcast each week. It's not the four easy payments of $37.25 that keep me away; rather, I fear the satellite dish might interfere with my powers of mental control, however diminished those abilities may be. Also, I will not purchase the on-demand video package from MLB.com to watch games on my computer, although for $14.95 per month or $79.95 for the entire season – less than fifty cents a game – it's like it's free.

And, I will no longer insist my kids learn how to sing the Mets fight song as a substitute for quality parenting, even though, to my ears, the line "Bring your kiddies, bring your wife, guaranteed to have the time of your life!" is so damn true it gives me a lump in my throat. In that vein, I will not pretend to have the stomach flu in order to skip the family trip to Cape Cod so I can focus on the Red Sox – Yankees series at Fenway Park this July. And I will resist, at all costs, the dangerous flirtation with Fantasy League Baseball, knowing full well that such a relationship could result in immediate revocation of computer privileges both at work and at home.

Also, I will encourage my children to view all professional sports as entertainment and remind them that losing one's hair or gaining weight or struggling with sleep are all related to their daddy inching one step closer to death rather than realizing his team will not win it all again this season. Finally, I will remind myself that next season's Opening Day is less than a year away, so no matter how bad this season turns out for the Red Sox or the Mets, there is always next season. Unless there's a strike – and if that's the case, I'm heading straight for the Peach Schnapps and the Patriots preseason.

HOW DONUTS SAVED MY LIFE

I learned my life's greatest lesson at the counter of a donut shop. I'd just finished the Boston Marathon, all 26.2 miles of it, and there in the Park Street T station, I bought two chocolate crullers and a glazed fritter, sat on the floor and ate. My marathon running career was over – ending not with a bang, not with a whimper, but with a stomach full of semi-stale pastries.

I'd been one of "them" for a while – one of those dedicated runners with their lean cheeks, taut legs, and bright, eager eyes filled with that sense of knowing something non-runners didn't know. I'd seen them on my daily three-mile trots – clustered in packs, softly chatting, in tune with each other's movements and pace. I wondered what secrets they shared. What truths had they discovered out there? Just what happened at Mile Four and beyond? Determined to find out, I ran a marathon. With one down, I set my sights on Boston.

I put in the daily miles and kept a log of how far I ran, where I ran, and how much water I drank. For my long runs, I smeared petroleum jelly all over my body, just like the real runners did. I caught bathroom breaks behind parked cars, just like they did. I slept a lot, stretched all the time, and ate mounds of pasta, just like they did. When Patriot's Day came, I ran the Boston Marathon, just like they did.

As the race began, I thought about what I was getting out of this whole experience, and my mind was a blank. I thought about the decision I'd made months before and wondered why I hadn't chosen something else, like swimming. Reminding myself of what I looked like in a Speedo reinforced that decision pretty quickly, so on I plodded, no closer to any real answers.

As the course stretched on, things got worse. I reached Wellesley College and detected a student's smirk. On Heartbreak Hill, I could have sworn a toddler laughed at me. Then, as I ran past Boston College towards the final stretch, I fell in next to an elderly runner methodically pounding away. Too short of breath to offer encouragement, I matched his strides, letting him know, for an old-timer, he was looking good, and I was there for him. He turned to me and said, "First time?" "Yep," I blurted.

"Thought so," he muttered as he kicked into overdrive, leaving me in his wake. If there was ever a sign I didn't belong running marathons, getting dusted by an octogenarian in Mile 22 ranks up there.

I finally crossed the finish line in the shadows of the Hancock Tower, and then it hit me. "Who *are* these people? And what am I doing here?" I was surrounded by my running brethren, those who'd cajoled and inspired me, but as I limped through the crowd, I realized I really was just a visitor - a stranger in a strange land.

I waddled on, looking for answers. I descended to the subway station below, and there they were – the answers I'd been seeking, racks and racks of glistening, moist pastries, beckoning me from their exercise-free, deep-fried world. "We're your real friends," they whispered to me from behind their glass cages. "Come join us and be happy."

Without hesitation, I slapped a sweaty five-spot on the counter, proclaiming, "I just ran 26.2 miles, so gimme two of those and one of them and a Boston Crème if you got one." I slumped to the floor with my bag of donuts, finally accepting the truth that I'd been kidding myself all along. For my entire marathon running career, all eighteen months of it, I never felt like I fit. The Vaseline applications always seemed a bit obscene, the long runs were like volunteering for dental surgery, and the only "runner's high" I ever got was when someone on the street corner yelled a greeting as I trundled by. I realized the only truth past Mile Three was that there was always another mile to run, nothing more, and nothing less.

Reaching into the bag for my second cruller, I decided I'd never again attempt a marathon. I'd finally figured out what they talked about on those epic runs – the fact that short, chubby guys with a penchant for pastries are not cut out to be marathoners. When they asked, "What are your splits?" or "Are you trying to qualify?" they really meant, "You'll never make it," and "You run like you've got a piano on your back." A long way to go to learn such simple truths.

So if you've ever considered joining the ranks of the marathoners, or if you're one yourself, perhaps gearing up for the big race, consider which road you'll take once the race is over. I took the road much more easily traveled – the road for the sometimes-in-shape, could-stand-to-lose-fifteen-pounds kind of guy. That guy who figured he'd rather belong to a world that's easier to see by car or TV than by running marathons. That guy who ran 26.2 miles and just wanted a few donuts and a ride home.

POUNDS OF BLAME

There is a crisis of corpulence in American today, and we tubbies need some help. It's not another fad diet we need, or more Richard Simmons in our lives. We just need someone to blame. We've tried losing the weight – honestly, we've tried really hard, but it's just not working. And we're running out of time. The news is all around us – we're getting fatter by the day. Two-thirds of us are overweight or obese, our kids are brushing their teeth with Jolt Cola, and even our pets can't fit into the outfits we bought them. We're quickly becoming One Nation Under MY GOD YOU'RE FAT! and unless we figure out who's responsible for the backs of our necks looking like a pack of bratwurst, we're only gonna look worse in our bathing suits this summer.

I, for one, am not going to sit around eating another bear claw and wait for the solution to waddle up to me. I'm getting out in front of this, and I've got the perfect approach - I'm gonna start acting like a smoker because no one plays the blame game better than our nation's smokers.

I've been watching the smokers - well, actually, the dead smokers' relatives - and I've learned one thing - it's not their fault! They may have purchased the cigarettes, they may have lit the cigarettes, and they may indeed have repeatedly smoked the cigarettes until they smelled like the back of a Turkish taxi cab, but someone else is to blame. The smokers and their crafty lawyers got so good at passing the blame that they hoodwinked the feds into strong-arming the tobacco companies into coughing up $200 billion to pay for their hacker-related maladies. Instead of laughing at the smokers, I think we can all learn a valuable lesson - it's okay to do really stupid things that ruin our health because it's not our fault.

A pack of healthy smokers in Louisiana has even taken the next bold step. These smokers are suing tobacco companies for potentially getting sick in the future. What an idea! Let's ignore the fact that suing for the chance that they may get sick is a lot like me grounding my four-year old daughter for dating her *potential* future boyfriend, Ray Ray, that dude who works the chairlift at Loon Mountain and lives with his step-uncle, raising sea monkeys for beer money. It may not be fair, but we porkers need to start doing the same.

Let's not kid ourselves. Our obsession with pre-processed non-dairy whipped dessert topping, double-stuffed triple-cheese meat lover's pizza, and hamper-sized Super Big Gulps isn't going away any time soon, so the faster we exit the Zone, leave South Beach for good, stop eating cabbage soup and start figuring out who is responsible for this fatness, the better off we'll all be.

For a guy who could lose more than a handful of pounds, this revelation could not have come at a better time. I've been what some have called "husky" my whole life, and I admit that I'd rather eat a sleeve of Ring Dings than take a walk around the block any day, so I'm wondering if there's someone to blame close by. How about my family? My siblings always hassled me about my weight, and my mom tried to solve every health-related issue with, "You must be hungry!" ("Help! My collarbone is broken!" "You'll be fine – have some polenta!") But lawsuits tend to ruin the holidays, so that's out.

Maybe I could blame the Chinese restaurant down the street for selling crab Rangoon and chicken fingers by the barrel. That had a lot to do with me hitting rock bottom last Christmas. I spent most of the holiday weekend dipping cold batter-fried chicken fingers into a small bucket of congealed duck sauce until I saw my reflection in the TV across the room. I wondered who was watching a documentary on the eating habits of the southeastern manatee, but, alas, the only sea cow in the room was me, and I started trying to take the blame for being a porky puke from that day on.

My attempt at accountability worked for a few months, but a man can eat only so much yogurt and drink only so many low-carb beers ("Michelob Ultra – Almost as Good as Liquid Styrofoam!"), and the weight is creeping back on – more like sprinting back on, actually. All the more reason to find out who's really responsible for my problem. And I'm not the first one to think like this. Last year a few parents claimed McDonalds was recklessly fattening up their kids. They went on Larry King to announce their plans to sue the Golden Arches, ranting and raving about how the Hamburgler is a pudge pusher, turning their teenagers into helpless blobs of miserable flesh. It was lost on the parents that their kids, sitting next to them, were popping glazed crullers into their mouths like Tic-Tacs. The lawsuits never went anywhere, but that Hamburgler, he's no dummy. McDonalds is experimenting with self-service kiosks for "easier" ordering, and I'm sure they'd let us cook the food if we all had our own hairnets.

I see that blaming a fast food restaurant for my problems is a lot like blaming the bank for bouncing a check. But the fact that I blew all my money on ponies and cheap booze is beside the point – they gave me the checks and the pen – how was I supposed to control myself? I don't have an answer to this quandary, but I plan on finding someone to blame soon – right after I finish this new pack of Camel no filters. I hear there's nothing better than a smoke after a Whopper Extra Value Meal, and it's not my fault if it tastes so good.

ASTRO-INSECURITY

It's easy to feel like an idiot these days. Reminders of my limited mental capacity swirl around me in a blizzard of stuff I don't understand. Each day I interact with things that force me to confront my inabilities. My television's remote control? No idea how it works. Dry cleaning? A real mystery. Cooking a burrito in the microwave for lunch? Nary a clue. And now I hear how NASA scientists landed a golf-cart sized robot in a sandy crater on the surface of Mars. Considering I can't drive a car with a stick shift, this Mars mission is a real blow to my self-esteem. I should be filled with pride, you're probably saying. Our ability to explore a distant planet in search of the remnants of water-enriched life and beam back color photos and chemical analyses of the surface might be cause for celebration for some, but it only reminds me that my VCR's clock still blinks "12:00 AM."

Knowing that our scientists will guide this robot, *Spirit*, to drive around the Martian landscape, looking at rocks, playing in the sand and generally showing the rest of the world that when it comes to unmanned dirt-digging and picture-taking robots, we Americans have no equal, may make you feel like a winner, but not me. I can't even explain why when it's a winter day in Boston, it's a summer night in Australia to an eight-year-old.

These NASA scientists are so good that another robot, *Opportunity*, landed on the opposite side of Mars from *Spirit* just the other day. The sports enthusiast in me likes to imagine this is the first step in next year's ratings hit, "Battle Bots from the Red Planet," but I think our nerdy pals have grander designs. You might ask what could be grander than billion-dollar American robots fighting on live TV from the surface of a strange world, and I'd have a hard time disagreeing, but I'm no scientist.

No scientist indeed! I may look like a scientist, with my pasty, semi-oily complexion and tight-fitting golf shirts, but that's where the similarities end. Frankly, I'd prefer that people brainy enough to pull off these Mars stunts were eight feet tall, mega-sized, draped in flowing brocaded robes, their enormous hairless skulls covered in pulsating veins, pumping blood to parts of the brain that I either don't have, can't find or killed off with whippets in Keith Moran's basement in tenth grade. That way, I could feel a little better about myself, with my normal pea-sized head, paying someone to change my car's oil and marveling at my "Hang in There Baby!" poster. ("Look out! Kitty's gonna fall!")

I'd also prefer them to sound a little different than me; when they talk, I want them to scream things like, "Earthlings, submit to our whims, or we will eat your glandular tissue for molecular energy," but their tone is disappointingly normal. It stinks that they sound just like Steve, the guy who sits next to me at work, except that when they talk, they say things like, "The telemetry of the radio-spectrometer will sync with the Global Satellite uplink to codify the regression transmission," and when Steve talks, he says things like, "Staplers are so useful," and "Hang in there baby!"

These scientists aren't the first ones to make me feel dumb. This summer a few British astrophysicists discovered a grouping of planets that resembles our own solar system. The following is a description of how they did such a thing: "The discovery was found by measuring the star's wobble caused by the gravity of the planet. The technique measures the very slight wobble of a central star and then uses the magnitude of this motion to determine the presence of orbiting planets, the size and shape of their orbits and their mass. The technique works only for larger planets and cannot detect those much smaller." And Timmy has two M's! Yippee!

But my time as a misinformed moron is about to end. I heard from the President the other day that there's a lot of space in our future, and I'm not going to be the only one left down here while someone else builds houses on the moon and gets a round-trip flight to Mars. This country's gonna need a whole crater of smart people, so it's time for me to hit the books, brush up on my quantum physics, astro-engineering, and Martian mining techniques. After a hard day of learning, I'll fall asleep on my teeny pillow, the light from the VCR's clock blinking across my face as I dream of digging holes with my new scientist pals on faraway planets. But until then, I'll be the stupid one hanging in there, baby!

DIAL M FOR MONKEY

Rumor has it our lawmakers are trying to stop us from using our cell phones while driving. Let me stop typing, pull over, and ponder that for a minute. Heck, I'm all for it! Various bills making the rounds in the State House advocate things like banning teenagers from instant messaging while talking on their cell phones during their driving test. Another bill enforces the buying and training of pet monkeys as passenger seat dialing assistants. Now *that's* an idea whose time has come. ("Dial Dominos, Mr. Whiskers!") I've swerved enough on the highway while checking my checking account balance on a phone keypad the size of a Saltine to realize I could use a hand. I support any law that combines safe driving with the grooming and training of monkeys, and with the proper instruction and wetnaps, this arrangement could work for all hominids across the nation.

There are signs that other Americans are making tough choices when it comes to cell phones. In fact, NASCAR just canned Winston Cigarettes after many years of marquee sponsorship in favor of NEXTEL, the cell phone company with the walkie-talkie option. That *was* a tough choice – driving and smoking makes sense to me; pretending to say, "Beam me up, Scotty" into your walkie-talkie while driving 180 mph doesn't. A cell phone company advocating the driving of really fast cars is like the corner liquor store sponsoring the local birthing hospital. ("This pregnancy brought to you by Old Duke Fortified Wine!")

I need a pet monkey to help me with my cell phone, considering it took me three years to figure out how to work the volume and store phone numbers. Until a few months ago, my typical conversation was something like this: "Hello? Hello? Can you hear me? Hello? Hold on – I have to get a pencil – what's your number again? Hello?"

Perhaps it's true that with the advance of personal technology comes greater anxiety. If this past Father's Day weekend was any indication, I agree.

For Father's Day, my wife went to Las Vegas for a bachelorette party. The centerpiece for the weekend was a visit to the popular Thunder Down Under All-Male Australian Cowboy Review. The concept is fascinating – collect the hunkiest bunch of Aussie range-ridin' studs you can find, ship them to America, and pay them to undress in front of my wife and her friends.

There are questions in life that beg the adage "Less is more," like how hot dogs are made or why the babysitter's trunk is filled with duct tape. As long as the hot dog tastes good and my kids are well-behaved, that's enough for me.

With that in mind, I went to sleep early Saturday night forgetting all about Bucky from Brisbane, content knowing my children were safe in their beds, dreaming of their mother's return. As my head hit the pillow, I had nary a recollection of that ad campaign for Las Vegas: "What happens here stays here."

That *is* a great sentiment, unless somehow your wife's cell phone accidentally dials home at 4 AM. I answered the phone, hearing shouts of, "Come on ladies! Let me hear you Sheilas make some noise," quickly followed by what sounded like feeding time at the kennel: "Wooo! Wooo! Wooo! Ohmygod! Ohmygod! Canhedothat? Hecandothat! Aroogah! Aroogah!"

I realized I had an ears-only seat at the after-dinner showing of the Thunder Down Under. I was riveted, straining to hear who'd actually placed the call and whether my wife was tipping sufficiently. Thanks to the wonders of cellular technology, I could almost smell the sweat and hear the shrieks. My wife and her friends were oblivious to the call, and I listened for five minutes, alternating between screaming, "Honey, pick up the phone!" and "Bucky, over here, over here! Bucky!" I finally hung up when I heard a woman yell, "I'm never going home! This is the best night of my life!"

I lay in bed, unable to fall back asleep, my mind wandering to the dusty Outback, my wife swept away by a strapping cowboy, his oiled muscles and shaven chest undulating with each stride of his flaxen-maned stallion in the shadow of Ayers Rock. In those early-morning hours of Father's Day, my mind became a blur of Harlequin Romance novels, divorce court and roaming charges. Glimpses of my future made real through a simple phone call.

If there was a need for a monkey trained to handle a tricky situation, my Father's Day experience proved it. Mr. Whiskers would have left the phone back in the hotel, focusing instead on protecting my best interests, remembering the important instructions, "Attack the buttocks, Mr. Whiskers!" But relying on a simian, no matter how well intentioned, would have proven a mistake. Few creatures that walk upright can resist the lure of naked Australian cowboys, and Mr. Whiskers would be no different. Besides, he'll be one busy monkey. I've got lots to learn about cell phone features, defensive driving and the latest dance moves from Down Under, and until he can recognize Bucky's phone number on caller ID, things just won't be right at home.

SPELLING ON STEROIDS

There are many things I hope my kids will do with their lives, and I'm not picky. Astronaut would be good; snake wrangler sounds exciting; high school graduate, spokesmodel, or maybe place-kicker for an Arena Football team would pass muster. I pray, however, that my kids never aspire to be champion spellers. Every spring, dozens of America's pre-teen spelling elite converge on our nation's capital to outspell each other and outwit the hapless adults who've agreed to referee the event.

After watching the bee on TV in the past, I vow to do my best to ensure my children never make the trip. I don't have anything against good spelling, but the National Spelling Bee is to good spelling what the Indy 500 is to good driving. It looks like driving, it sounds like driving, but normal driving doesn't require helmets, a pit crew and a fence to contain flying shards of flaming auto parts.

The National Spelling Bee is not normal spelling – it's spelling on steroids. For fifteen rounds, well-groomed, pint-sized spell-it-alls slug it out over words like hypozeuxis and gnathonic as their parents and spelling coaches fret, squeal and videotape the event for posterity. To compare, my eight-year old is learning how to spell frolic, picnic, and donkey while those kids are nailing words like boudin, symphily, and dipnoous. Inviting a donkey to frolic at a picnic sounds like fun; inviting a friend with a case of symphily in his dipnoous to share his boudin in your backyard is not my idea of a good time – keep that kid away from the potato salad, I say.

The key lesson I learned from watching it is that no one seems to want to spell anything! The basic strategy employed by these wee wizards of the dictionary was to delay spelling the word put to them by asking a series of pointed, obnoxious questions of the judge, who looked like what I imagine Droopy Dog would look like as a moderator of a nationally televised spelling tournament. Each contestant paused, delayed, and frustrated everyone in the auditorium and at home by haggling over everything. "Did the word pass through French?" "Was it Anglicized?"

"What's the word's origin?" "Can you use it in a sentence?" "Are there any other meanings?"

Moderator Droopy looked like he was ready for a nap by the middle of the tenth round, but he patiently responded to each question. As questions go, I guess I should hope my kids are smart enough to get that far. "Does the word have a Greek origin?" is a bit better than, "Do you want fries with that?" or "When am I eligible for parole?" but still, I'd rather not have my kids aspire to eggheaded greatness when there are picnics to plan.

I'll admit part of this bias is the fact I'm nursing a twenty-year old spelling grudge. As a sixteen year old, I had my shot at greatness. I'd just won Chaminade High School's junior class spelling bee, crushing my competition en route to the finals, to be beamed via close-circuit TV to the 2,000 students across the entire school. I spent days preparing, pouring over dictionaries, attacking stacks of flash cards, memorizing word roots, word origins and derivations.

As the finals approached, I was pumped – so pumped that on the first word of the contest, I froze, panicked and fell apart, misspelling the word "belfry" with two "l's." I remember an eruption of laughter as I bungled the word, and I quickly snaked off-camera, back to homeroom, defeated, deflated, and ashamed. My chance for victory got stuck in a misspelled belfry, and I never made much of an effort to be the best speller around after that.

So I'd rather let my kids succeed or fail in other things. Telling a group of people you'd been cut from an Arena Football team sounds so much cooler than explaining that, "If it wasn't for the confusion over the origin of the prefix, I had 'rhathymia' in the bag." True, champion spellers are winners in their own right, and their parents love them just as much as I love my kids, but I need to be comforted that my children will struggle with things other than spelling words that no one will ever actually use. But if they do make the decision to go the route of the champion speller, I'll wish them my best, but I won't be making the trip to Washington. My picnic schedule's filling up, and someone's got to frolic with the donkey.

CONFESSIONS OF A
FORMER CLASS SECRETARY

My career as a class secretary is over, and it's time for me to come clean. I was a class secretary for Middlebury College's Class of 1989, and I was a liar. My role of class secretary was an unglamorous one. My job was to collect tidbits of news from my classmates and craft quarterly reports on their successes, to be printed in my school's alumni magazine. From the day I was elected to the position, I had a lingering sense that class secretary was one rung below society columnist and half a rung above fact checker for the community real estate circular, but I accepted the role with vigor.

I'm not sure when I started playing with the truth, but once I started, I couldn't stop. I could claim I inserted untruths into the Class Notes after growing weary reading about my charity-organizing fighter pilot classmate who ran a marathon in Anchorage, or how the disease-curing architect moonlighted as a pastry chef while attending law school on the weekends. After graduation, I was living in my parents' basement, clipping coupons for Raman Noodle soup, eking out a career as an underpaid elementary school teacher, so maybe the comparisons took their toll.

The trick was to make the job sound just real enough without being totally outlandish. Consider Dorothea H's dual life – she "works days as a crane operator for a Japanese construction firm in NY and plays the accordion in West Side clubs at night," (Summer '92). Or the supposed demanding schedule of Graham G, "short-order cook at fashionable east-side eatery and hand model for the Ford Agency," (Winter '92). How about Mark D's collection of poems about his life as a dancer in Kuala Lumpur titled, *Alone I Wiggle*, mentioned in the Spring '92 issue - "While in Indonesia [false], Mark ran into Ernie S, then in law school [true], who'd just returned from teaching baseball to Montagnard tribesmen in the hills of Laos [false]."

John R sent me an imaginary note while working in Manhattan, bragging, "Looking down the barrel at 40k! You talk high finance, you're talking to Johnnie!" (Summer '92), soon followed by Mike S's pretend note in the Winter '92 issue while attending law school, "I can't wait to be the big bad bear in the courtroom so I can feed those prosecutors the bagel." That didn't even make any sense, but it sounded kind of funny.

The lies peaked in that Winter '92 issue when I created a classmate from thin air. "Wade Peters penned a short note after returning from his 18-month tour around the world, claiming the surf had never been better in Bali. He ran into Haydn C in a Bangkok disco, writing, 'We partied it up, and then I cruised off into the jungle to check out how Buddhists celebrate the holidays. Man, do we have a lot to learn . . . .'" Haydn was real, but Wade was not. I had grand plans for him, but despite repeated attempts, Wade never emerged from the jungle, not to appear in the Class of '89 Notes again.

Soon after, I mentioned two works by Sean B that got me into hot water. The magazine's editor wrote me a letter in April '93 that demanded a halt to my flexibility with the truth. He wrote, "Sean's *Kama Sutra of Cleveland* and *Knock Hockey Nightmares* sound fascinating, but unless he really is writing a thesis and a novel, you don't want to say he is. On the other hand, saying that someone's dream is to treat Sasquatch for athlete's foot is okay, because it's obviously a joke." Frankly, I can't imagine any classmate not thinking anything titled *Kama Sutra of Cleveland* to be anything but a joke; then again, I wasn't the one responsible for journalistic integrity. The editor continued, "It's like the clock that strikes 13; it throws into question everything that's gone before. Eventually is becomes hard for us (or your readers) to know where the jokes stop and the facts begin."

I'd broken the basic rule of all journalists, paid and unpaid, by weaving real and imagined facts together. But can you blame me? Who wants to read about your recent appointment as Recording Secretary to the Kiwanis Club of Greater Altoona when we could be reading about Steve B's marriage to '60's comedy icon and *Laugh-In* star Ruth Buzzi, or Tim O's study of the art of Indonesian hand puppetry? "They liberate me," Tim was quoted in the Summer '92 issue.

With the College's rebuke in mind, I kept it clean for a while, but old habits die hard. Between the Summer '94 and Winter '00 issues, Tom D's career took an interesting and semi-true turn; he not only played guitar in his band, Jabberwocky Dream [not true] while working for Jeb Bush's gubernatorial campaign [true], but Tom also spent three months in the Chilean jungle as a "member of an MIT-based research team examining the impact of urban sprawl on indigenous cultures" [false]. He really was living at his parents' house [true] listening to his Van Halen records while waiting to get his second graduate degree [true].

But just as the string eventually runs out on all liars, mine ran out after fifteen years, not from the falsehoods, but from my classmates growing tired of reading about the same twenty people and their accomplishments, real or fake. My classmates voted me out in a somewhat disputed, beer-soaked election at our last reunion.

Yes, I admit it, Ryder S did not work for Beaniemania.com, an online clearinghouse for buyers and sellers of collectibles (Winter '02); Sean B never ran the Potter's Wheel, a pottery shed and book exchange (Winter '01); and Erik V's career as a member of the Tulane University Green Larks barbershop quartet (Summer '96), manager of Whittle Works, a crafts cooperative, (Fall '96) and author of the best-selling novel, *Night of the Squirrel* (Fall '91) never happened, at least, for real.

For me, it's back to the real world, where most of us don't write novels or spend months in the jungles of Asia. But I did recently read that Victoria H is managing a San Francisco candle emporium – Wax On Wax Off (Spring '04), and I'm hoping she's still hiring.

THIS ELECTION BROUGHT TO YOU BY THE HIGHEST BIDDER

With only 300 shopping days left until the 2004 Presidential Election, it's time to stop thinking about Janet Jackson's choice of body jewelry and pay more attention to just who'll be our next president. And based on the non-stop coverage of every waking moment of the primary season so far, paying attention won't be the problem. By this November, you'll have the American political process rammed down your throat so often you'll be humming "Hail to the Chief" in your sleep. Elections, like the Olympics, are a funny thing. For three years we could not care less about someone's love of the spotted owl or her synchronized swimming routine, but at the first note of the Olympic theme song or the mention of the word "caucus," we obsess over the most minute details of either contest, dying to see if that Chinese diver nailed the Triple Lindy or what that candidate *really* meant when he said, "tax cuts." ("Did he mean tax CUTS or TAX cuts?")

For me, the presidential race isn't much of a choice - Republicans and Democrats are kind of like choosing between paper and plastic at the supermarket. What I'd rather see is true choice in American politics, like choosing between the cross-dressing dance instructor who wants to outlaw cheese and the burly lumberjack who supports a free education for all mammals. ("No ruminant left behind!") Now *that* would be a race! But in the end, all we get is two white guys with family money trying to convince us that the other guy will leave us vulnerable to invasion by Quebec.

As with the Olympics, the outcome of our four-year national elections is wholly dependent on money. Most Olympic medals are won by a handful of well-fed, well-funded countries, or at least those that divert enough money from their transportation departments to field a quality squad. Similarly, in our national elections, the winners always have the deepest pockets and the best coaches. Face it – by the time we finish these primaries, Al Sharpton will resemble a North Korean water polo player, sitting on the sidelines with a deflated ball and a fat lip, an ill-fitting bathing suit from 1987 stretched across his flabby waist. Likewise, come summertime, John Kerry will look like a prima donna US sprinter, gliding into the starting blocks with a cocky swagger, his slavish coaches and assistants waiting with an American flag and bottled water on the sidelines.

Sadly, so few of us actually vote; I bet twice as many Americans tune in to watch the hammer throw once every four years than vote for president. But I think I have the cure to what ails us. What the American political process needs is some truth – not in the Howard Dean primal howl for attention way, but in the way our politicians embrace the dollar. It's about time we encourage our politicians to flaunt the flow of money into their campaigns. Everyone knows no one gets elected to any position of prominence without lots of cash, so why not be up-front about it? Let's get rid of "soft money" funneling through a shady lifelong political backroom hack or through mysterious donations to the "Friends for American Trust and Perseverance Political Action Committee."

Instead, let's convince our leaders to brag about their endorsements while they strut around DC in their logo-covered suits, like European soccer players or NASCAR drivers. Picture it now – Minnesota Senator

Mark Dayton with a huge Target sticker on his lapel, or New Jersey Senator Frank Lautenberg with an ADP ball cap on his head, or Vice-President Cheney with a tee shirt that reads, "My ex-co-workers at Halliburton ripped off the Army for millions and all I got was this Lousy Tee Shirt."

The House Chamber could sell its naming rights and billboard space, and corporations could sponsor important legislative events, like cloture votes and the State of the Union address - "This filibuster brought to you by the Little Blue Pill. Stand firm with Viagra." The Speaker of the House would say things like, "The chair recognizes the Kraft Foods Representative from Wisconsin," or "My esteemed colleague from the Tyson-chicken-eating district of Arkansas has the floor."

Money would come out of the closet, free to marry any politician to any cause, profit or non. Vermont Independent Representative Bernie Sanders may look for the Sierra Club's sponsorship while Colorado Republican Ben Campbell might seek out the liquor industry for underwriting. ("Night Train for Nighthorse!")

The buying and selling of political influence would be as transparent as the daily activity on the floor of the New York Stock Exchange. Greater truth would generate more money, which would then foster better competition, forcing our leaders to produce or perish, quickly finding themselves back at home watching the hammer throw reruns on late-night cable like the rest of us. As for actual votes, they would quickly become less relevant. Your time at the supermarket or at the new car showroom would have far more to do with who gets sent to Washington than would your single, lonely, non-revenue-generating vote.

But the best part of getting more money into politics would mean even more money for corporations, which would give our Olympic teams that extra edge. And I, for one, will do whatever it takes to see our rhythmic gymnastics team finally bring home the gold. This is a country for winners, no matter how much it costs.

WHO'S YOUR DADDY?

There are disturbing reports out of Florida that Santa's cover may be blown. Apparently, a dim-witted first-grade teacher spilled the beans about the Tooth Fairy, which led to a frank discussion with her students about the realities of sled travel and gift delivery in the world today. I can't fault the teacher, after making the huge mistake myself this summer while reading the last page of Judy Blume's *Fudge and the Unnecessary Sequel,* where Fudge and his brother Peter have a heart-to-heart about the Tooth Fairy. I'd suspected that my son Sam, now eight years old, had already stopped believing, but based on the shrieks and tearful wailing, he hadn't. The scary thing was that he immediately asked about Santa, wanting to know if he was "a fake too." I assured him Santa was listening at that very moment, and one more comment like that would prove disastrous for this year's holiday season.

But I think Santa's Day of Reckoning is fast approaching in our house. The questions really started last December, when Sam asked, "What if an elf wants to do something different with his life than just make toys for other people?" I tried to dismiss his concerns with the standard response: "Santa knows when you annoy Daddy with silly questions. He sees everything." Sam was undeterred, jumping quickly to questions about how Santa makes his reindeer fly. I went for the standard "Santa uses magic" line in response, adding, "and everyone knows *that*."

"Uh huh, Santa magic," Sam replied quietly, and then he paused a bit before launching into a soliloquy on Christmas Eve snacking: "Reindeer don't like carrots or graham crackers. It makes them ill. Also, never put milk out because they can get sick. Santa will eat pretty much anything you leave out, like a sandwich or cookies, and I don't think it's a good idea to leave beer like you did last year. If he drinks a beer at every house he could get arrested and then no one would get anything."

The boy had a good point, although Santa'd certainly have time to sober up over Provo. I waited for the next slew of questions – about a big enough sleigh, sleep deprivation issues, houses with no fireplaces, you know, the usual stuff, but Sam stopped there, and I feared he was onto me.

I can remember the Christmas when I learned the truth about Santa. It was a week or so before the big day. I'd already mailed my annual list of demands, and I was waiting to hear back. In our town, we'd get a crudely written mimeographed form letter back from Santa, written, I now realize, by the postal interns who'd failed the mailroom vacuuming tests. Sentences like, "Ease up on the pricey stuff kid – it ain't like you're the only one celebrating Christmas," or, "Expect the unexpected on the morning of Christmas," which always made me anticipate Santa's henchmen making a visit to reclaim all the toys I didn't deserve but got anyway.

As I waited for Santa's response, my mom surprised me with a letter she dug out of her purse, declaring, "Oh, I got this at the post office this morning. It's for you! It's from Mrs. Claus!" I looked at the envelope and thought I recognized my mom's handwriting, but she hovered over me, expecting me to open it, which I did.

The letter was very specific, noting how I'd certainly requested quite a bit, and how wanting a Johnny Bench Batter-up, although ambitious, wasn't a possibility this year, "due to some warehousing issues my husband is having." I scanned the letter for confirmation that the Planet of the Apes tree-house would indeed be mine this year, and all seemed okay. But as I scrutinized the signature, I smelled a holly-scented rat. That signature was my mother's – no question about it. I'd learned to forge it for my sisters' detention notices months before, and I could sign it myself with a grand flourish. I realized that either my mother was two-timing my dad with Mr. Claus or she was desperately trying to keep the Christmas dream alive for me. I opted for the latter, feigned ecstatic excitement at Mrs. Claus's response and escaped to my room, despondent over the truth that Santa was bogus. All of it – lies. The Island of Misfit Toys? – not a shred of truth. Kris Kringle and the Burghermeister Meisterburgher? – pure phonies. The four empty beer cans, half-eaten cookies and reindeer urine on the carpet? – all my dad's fault.

That Christmas morning was miserable. Sure, I got the tree-house with M-16- toting mandrills, but something was missing. I realize now what was missing was the belief that these board games, action figures, and Tyco Race Tracks were given by a generous, jolly stranger who saw all the good and bad things I did and still found it in his heart to give me gifts - *not* from my parents who knew I was a pain in the ass! My mom and dad had heaps of evidence of my pissy moods, my love for argument and my selfish ways, yet I still got tons of loot.

What was missing that morning was the belief in generosity for the sake of joy; instead, I was stuck with the lasting realization that I was a greedy fool who'd been getting more than I deserved from parents who'd been culturally dragooned into feeding the gift-giving beast every December.

It's one thing to think Santa was a forgiving fellow who lived to make kids happy. It's another to think my parents had to hire a babysitter to drive to the store to buy this stuff with their hard-earned money, and they weren't even getting credit for it. Merry Christmas to you, our flabby little complainer.

A few nights ago my son asked to write an email to Santa. The email began, "Dear Santa, how was your summer? Were you chosen to be Santa by Jesus? Say a nice 'thank you' to your elves." The Jesus comment might have been a hint, but Sam quickly launched into a laundry list of needs and wants, stopping just short of asking for a Shetland pony that could do his math homework, so I knew the Santa Secret was safe for a little while longer.

And even if Sam did find the things I had bought him hidden in the closet and just happened to ask for the same exact things in his email to Santa, we still have his three-year-old sister to work with. To date, Maisie's only interest in Santa is her insistence that she has two daddies – Santa and me. Although a great sitcom idea, there is no truth to that statement. When I try to lay claim to her bloodline she runs off, taunting, "Santa is my daddy. Santa is my daddy." So until I figure out how to handle that issue, I'll just have to trust in the Rankin-Bass propaganda machine and proclaim that Santa does indeed exist. It's always easier to believe in something when there are gifts involved, and those should keep coming for the foreseeable future.

But the year we're running a little low on holiday cash, the first person I'm calling for a short-term loan is Maisie's other dad up north. He'd better come through, or I'm taking him, his wife and all the elves down with me.

LIVE FREE OR DIE, ANIMALS, DIE!

I was welcomed to New Hampshire by gunfire. I'd been a resident for ten minutes when, standing in my driveway amid boxes and furniture, inhaling my first breath of home ownership, I heard the gunshots. Looking across the street, I spotted a man, my new neighbor, cradling a single-barrel shotgun, smoke rising from the muzzle, calmly approaching a small animal spinning in erratic circles on the ground. The man looked like Outlaw William Munney, Clint Eastwood's character from *Unforgiven*, right when Clint's decided he really *is* a murdering, blood-thirsty monster.

My own Mr. Munney paused right above the tiny critter, reloaded, took aim, and blasted Chip or Dale into the sultry June sky. He saw me across the street, waved hello and walked back inside. I guess a plate of cookies no longer says "Welcome to the Granite State" like a driveway flecked with rodent grey matter does, and I hadn't realized New Hampshire changed its motto to, "Live Free or Die, Chipmunk Die!" But I was here in my own house, finally, and I was ready for any challenge.

Eleven years to the day of my wedding, my wife, two kids and I moved into our first home, leaving the gilded servitude of a Massachusetts boarding school campus for the leafy city of Concord, New Hampshire, my wife's hometown and the place we decided to set down roots.

Moving north was easy – the tough part was saying goodbye to six years of free living. I'd gotten used to no rent, free food, tennis courts at the ready, ice skating at my command, and the cacophony of twenty-five high school girls living outside my door. In fact, the silence was what kept me up at night in my new house. I couldn't sleep at all that first week, missing the reassuring tones of, "Mrs. O'Shea, I'm out of vodka!" or the popular rhetorical question, "Does Febreeze work on bong water?" coming from the hallways. All I heard now were the crickets, the wind, and, sadly, hordes of mice invading my kitchen.

The mice needed to go. Resisting the urge to phone Mr. Munney for advice, I bought glue traps, taking matters into my own hands. Those of you who think glue traps are cruel, wishing I'd used the traditional snap-the-neck type, should realize I never expected to catch a single mouse, and glue traps were the best way not to lose a finger in the process. The next morning I found two poor creatures stuck in the glue, staring at me with huge dark eyes, their rodent snouts whimpering for mercy. What was I supposed to do now? I reminded myself that a homeowner must take action, so I grabbed the mice and their traps and dropped them in the bottom of the garbage barrel in the garage. I knew it was a cowardly thing to do, letting them starve to death like that, but I hoped the rotting skulls of these unlucky two would put all other mice on notice.

Apparently, my lesson was ignored, as I caught another the next morning. But this time I never hesitated, running outside and stomping on it, snuffing out its life. I thought I heard a mutter of approval from Mr. Munney across the way, my critter-killin' cred intact, but then again, it was probably the dead mouse's soul limping its way past me on the way to Rodent Purgatory.

The mice were gone, but I had bigger problems. Our lawn out back was riddled with huge ground-burrowing hornets, the trees were filled with cobwebs the size of Kirstie Alley's bloomers, and the carpenter ants congregating in my dining room were so big I swear they wore tool belts. To make things worse, I learned that moles had dug an elaborate system of tunnels in the backyard, turning my lawn into a series of ridges, bumps and curves, making it look like a grassy back of a beached Humpback whale and about half as useful.

Even the neighbors who aren't varmint vigilantes do their best to remind me of my new-found situation. "Donner the Neighbah" approached me and my kids one morning as we sat in the open hatch of our car, waiting to head out for the weekend. She wasted no time telling us about the neighborhood menagerie. "There was a huge moose across the street the other day," Donner began, "and we got foxes that are big and wicked aggressive. And the coyotes will make you want to keep any pets you have inside. The wild turkeys won't attack unless you look at them, but other than that, it's a real safe neighborhood."

Of course, Donner tells this to two children who have nightmares about My Pretty Pony. My kids sat in shocked silence until she told them about the local black bear that'd eat any dog it saw "like a little snack." Both kids gasped, imagining a 400-pound animal treating a litter of newborn puppies like a box of chocolates. My children, afraid of butterflies and sparrows, now had to live with the fear of a marauding bear lurking in the garage, ready to pounce as they search in vain for their anti-bear bike sirens. As Donner walked away, I realized the purpose of home ownership. It's *not* to build equity, provide for my family, or even have a nice place to sleep – it's to wage war against the natural world, to prevent living things other than your immediate family from entering and, God forbid, staying for any length of time. "Kill or be inconvenienced" is the motto, and I shout it with all my might.

Once I saw the truth, I figured the best way to stem the tide of nature's onslaught was to buy a dog. But with any major homeland defense purchase, there are consequences. First, the dog's pee wreaked havoc, making our lawn look like it needed a heavy dose of Porcelana Age Cream to hide those embarrassing brown spots. Then, Brady, who can best be described as a well-fed pre-teen wearing a tiny gorilla costume, destroyed all shrubs and bushes that might provide cover for the turkey attack Donner warned us about.

But Brady didn't stop at deforestation. With the snow's final retreat this spring, he dug a hole so deep I found him gnawing on Chairman Mao's neck bone the other day. Just this weekend, Brady carved a series of crop circles in the shape of pork chops into the part of the lawn that's not been claimed by the MTA (Mole Transit Authority).

However, the thought of hungry alien canines massing in the skies above, drawn to my home by Brady's pork-inspired landscaping, doesn't worry me. I've kept up relations with Donner, saved up a healthy stack of glue traps, and have Mr. Munney's phone number on speed dial. And if the dogs descend, the bear attacks, or the angry ghosts of murdered mice decide to exact revenge, we can always escape down into the mole tunnels. Even better, I hear there are some lovely apartments for rent downtown. Interested in buying a house?

LIONEL RICHIE WON'T MEND A BROKEN HEART

I sit in the back of a taxi taking me to the train station for the commute home. It's winter, the streets covered in slush as wet snow smears the cab's windows. I'm alone in the car, save the driver; we move in silence, the ride only a short distance. The driver turns on the radio, and I hear Lionel Richie's voice sing, "Hello, is it me you're looking for . . . ," and now it's the three of us alone in this cab, the driver, Lionel and me. The break in silence prompts me to ask, "So, the Commodores were never the same once Lionel left, huh?" It was then my driver turned and told me what this song meant to him.

He explained as he drove, telling me "Hello" was the song playing on the radio the moment he set eyes on the most beautiful woman in the world. He fell in love immediately, and soon after, my driver and the woman were planning their lives together, thinking about coming to America to find a new life, their love the foundation for anything the future held. He told me "Hello" fills him with joy.

At this point, I too was filled with joy, buoyed by the idea that kindred spirits are everywhere, the two of us bound in a mutual appreciation for the power of popular music. But as we approached the curb outside the station, I asked him, "Did you two get married?"

"No," he replied, turning the radio off. He told me how their love had ended badly, how his older brother had stolen the girl away, crushing his happiness, forcing him to leave his country and come to America alone. "My heart is filled with blackness for my brother," he said. This happened in 1983, and he hadn't spoken to his brother since. "I think of the two of them a lot. I am sad thinking of them."

With that, I paid the fare and turned to go, but as I shut the door to leave, he exclaimed, "But Kenny Rogers, he fills me with rage! The song 'Lady' makes want to repay my brother in blood." Now this was something completely different, and I climbed back into the cab to listen.

He explained that "Lady" was the song he listened to the last night he and his girlfriend spent together, the two of them lying in bed, as *he* dreamt of being her knight in shining armor and *she* plotted when to fold them, when to walk away and when to run off with his brother.

My driver discovered the truth about their relationship the next morning. He left for America immediately, toting a miserable soundtrack of sappy '80s love songs burned into his memory, Lionel and Kenny forever reminding him of stolen love and fractured fraternal bonds. For a second, I thought about telling him that whenever I hear "Lady," I think about fried chicken, liposuction and Dolly Parton, enough to produce a mild case of dyspepsia and a fear of chicken grease on my shirt, but not enough to make me want to batter-fry my brother. But I decided against it.

I wished my driver good luck, shut the door and ran off as the snow continued down. And I imagined a woman, halfway across the world, listening to Lionel Richie, holding back the tears she wishes she could cry as snow falls outside her window.

A SONG TO MYSELF

For most of my life, I've been a bit of a worrier, someone whose idea of a relaxing weekend was reorganizing his sock drawer, cataloguing his batteries by type and brand, and waking up at 5:30 on Sunday morning, his mind too full of what Monday held to appreciate sleeping in. Some have called me the opposite of calm stoicism, high-strung, a stress case, and nervous wreck. And I was never in a position to disagree, too worried about picking up the dry cleaning or paying my bills to make much of an argument otherwise. But I have a story to tell you, a story that changed my life and my worry-filled ways.

In the early fall of 2003, I saw Bruce Springsteen at Fenway Park in Boston, the first concert of its kind at the storied home of the Red Sox. It was quite an event - the park was transformed - an enormous stage filled deep center field, and seats covered the grass. The ticket, hard to come by, was a gift from my friends Peter and Kathleen, and as thousands of us poured into the park for the show, smiling, slightly boozed and ready to sing along at the tops of our lungs, I had no idea I was hours away from stumbling across the secrets of my universe.

But let's get something very clear – I'm not a crazy BRUUUUCE fan – my "Born to Run" tattoo was temporary, I don't dream about vacationing in the swamps of Jersey, and I stopped playing with my E Street Band action figures once "Tunnel of Love" hit the airwaves. I was not someone who thought seeing Bruce at Fenway was like spotting the Virgin Mary at Fatima – I wanted to have fun and forget my troubles for a night, not look to the healing powers of the second verse of "Thunder Road" for what might ail me.

But I do love the music and admit to wanting to see Bruce at some point in my lifetime. The show did not disappoint. Bruce rocked for more than three hours, he and his band playing lots of their great songs, the crowd singing along to every word. At one point, Bruce told us how on this night he'd perform a rock and roll exorcism, thinly alluding to the struggles the Sox had had over the years against the Yankees in this park. Bruce told us he'd use music to shake the ghosts away.

As the concert neared its end, something happened to me. I'm not sure what it was; maybe the watery keg beer, or the sublime music, or maybe it really was the ghosts of all those Red Sox disappointments that had been swirling around the stadium for so many years. But whatever it was, I couldn't contain myself. At the first hint of "Rosalita," a song from one of Bruce's early albums in the '70's, I jumped from my seat way above home plate and ran down to a tiny platform hanging over the right field railing. The sounds of the organ swept into the drums, bass and guitar, quickly followed by the saxophone and horns, and then Bruce's voice pleaded with his girlfriend to sneak out with him for a little summertime fun. And I started dancing – completely alone in a sea of people.

Within seconds I was lost in the music – I could feel my body move to every note as I sang along, knowing all the words. At one point I remember holding on to the railing and leaping up as the song built to a crescendo, ". . . and your poppa says he knows that I don't have any money," as the band and the crowd clapped in perfect syncopation. The song surged forward to that point where everyone yells "HEY" sixteen times, the music rising and peaking to a climax, the band and the crowd united in a shout to the sky.

At that moment, as I jammed my fists in the air and screamed along with everyone else, I was awake, aware and alive like I'd never been before. And it hit me - this was my declaration to me - my celebration of me and my time on this planet – in Fenway Park, with Bruce loud as hell, my belly full of beer, my body drenched in sweat, losing all sense of anyone and anything else. For the first real time in my life, I wasn't a son, brother, husband, father, friend, fan, co-worker, customer, taxpayer, boss or buddy – I was just me and me alone, and I was free.

Someone once described for me what it means to find the divine for the first time. He described it as a visceral, immediate, emotional punch to the senses that knocked him flat, wrenching him from his ordinary life and making him a believer. Those five minutes were like that – like an aural slap seared into my memory that I can't shake, an awakening to me, myself and I. If that's what finding religion is all about, then at Fenway Park, in the right field upper box seats, in the midst of thousands of strangers, I was ordained as the one and only Minister to the Church of Me, ordained by my own dance-fueled sweat. As the song ended, I turned around and saw an entire row of people cheering, a group of women I'd never seen before in my life applauding me as I bounded back to my seat, a smile on my face ear to ear.

Since that night, I've grown to see I'll never have enough money or enough security, and I'm certain I'm only getting shorter, fatter and balder as I approach my forties. I'll never be the best parent, the nicest neighbor, the most generous giver, and I'll never make up for the careless and calculated things I've done to others and to myself, but I can't change that. What I discovered was the richness of everyday life that's always surrounded me, and I needed to recognize, appreciate and hold on to it. I realized I was letting it slide on by, too consumed with worrying about things I couldn't control. "Rosalita" taught me how to grab hold with both hands and never let go.

I found out something about myself that night that I'll carry with me forever – that I believe in the power of me, that I get one shot at life, and I better get busy making the most of it.

JESUS IN MY HEART
AND IN MY LUNCH

Let's be honest – Jesus is a lousy boyfriend. I don't fill my chalice from that jug of wine, if you know what I'm saying, but even so, Jesus and I need some help. I'm the one doing all the calling, asking all the questions, *making the effort*, and Jesus doesn't even look my way. I've learned to live with the missed birthdays, the unanswered prayers for X-ray vision, even the feeling that it's always my fault, but it still doesn't make things right. As if I have enough self-confidence not to need a little attention in return for everything I'm doing to keep this relationship from falling apart! We all need validation now and again, and Jesus acts like he's all that and a bag of rosary beads.

Not everyone in my family feels the same way. My six-year old daughter, Maisie, is convinced Jesus can do no wrong. Not a day goes by that she doesn't mention how she and Jesus have something special, always finding just the right moment to remind us about what they share.

Standing in line at Wal-Mart, Maisie announced, "Jesus is a good person," and "I think Jesus will be my husband. He is a special man." This is all well and good and may indeed be true, but not when you're holding a five pound feedbag of generic cheese puffs and a toilet plunger while the other customers start to smile in a "God's last name is not 'Dammit'" kind of way. There's not much to do at that point except hum the opening bars of "Onward Christian Soldiers" and hope no one invites us to a 700 Club Bean Supper.

This past summer, my wife and daughter were in the house in the late afternoon when an intrepid pair of Mormons approached the door. My wife had bragged for years how, if ever given the chance, she'd invite the Mormons in and demonstrate that a life without caffeine and cold beer is no life at all. But as the Mormons reached the front step, my wife froze. When asked about her relationship with Christ, she explained that we were a strict Catholic family and had no need for anything else, prompting one of the missionaries to say, "That's okay. It's wonderful to know that Jesus lives in your heart." Maisie, in the next room and to this point oblivious to the situation, heard the mention of Jesus in someone else's heart and tore around the corner, announcing, "JESUS! Jesus is in my heart! Jesus is my BEST friend!" The Mormons hesitated for a second, thinking this might be the proverbial foot in the door, but my wife thwarted the move, mumbling something about "Praise the Lord" and shutting the door. I imagined my daughter screaming at the window, pleading with the LDS reps to save her from this Godless house while my wife hushed her up with a Diet Coke and a few rum-filled candies. Instead, they went outside, where Maisie spent the next fifteen minutes shouting at the two missionaries as they made their way to every house on our block, "I still love Jesus! If you see him, tell him I'm gonna marry him!"

Good for her – if he'd been listening, Jesus would've caught a tiny boost of self-confidence, and we all know a happy boyfriend has lots of self-confidence. As I once read in *Reader's Digest*, it's hard to love anyone else when you don't love yourself. Maybe that's what's making Jesus such a cruddy boyfriend – he needs a little dose of self-love to recharge his batteries and get our relationship back on track.

And I've got just the idea. I know Jesus has another birthday coming up this year, and I'm planning ahead. Rather than a bunch of whispery prayers or meandering lamentations, I'm giving Jesus a few pointers – advice that will improve his approach, his appeal and his brand. He'll never make this partnership work unless he makes the effort to turn things around. My three-part plan is just what Jesus needs to start playing an equal role in this crazy little thing called eternal and forgiving love, and for him to start being the man I know he can be.

First, it's time to ditch the "deus ex machina" and go for some "deus ex media." Jesus needs to let us know he's out there. We don't need more signs – we have them in spades. What we need is for Jesus to pre-empt all local programming and deliver a well-written, humorous, yet informative explanation on where he's been and what he's been up to. While he's at it, he could let us in on a few secrets, like what's the deal with the Bermuda Triangle, explain why Whoopi Goldberg is famous, and does he prefer boxers, briefs or a loin cloth.

Maybe I could get him to take questions from the audience. I have one from my son I could use a little help with, actually. About five years ago Sam asked me, "So if God can do anything he wants, why does he make bad people?" Five-year olds don't want a discourse on St. Thomas Aquinas's polemic on the incorruptibility of the human soul – that's about as appealing as watching Barney the Purple Dinosaur and mommy having a naked wrestle punch fight on pay-per-view, and that was the only answer that came to mind. I still don't have much of a response, but I bet Jesus does. Jesus could carve out a few minutes of his speech to explain just how all those Philadelphia Eagles fans and Boston drivers serve a purpose in his master plan.

Next, Jesus needs to start building a winning team. No one wants to date the coach of a last-place squad. It's bad enough the alumni stopped caring and let the spazzy kiddy ticklers take all the starting spots, but Jesus will never compete and land the top recruits unless he improves his approach. I know. I was one of those potential players, and I have to admit, the assistant coach's official visit and sales pitch were lacking.

I was sixteen, at Catholic school, getting ready for my last real summer of high school before senior year, when I was approached by one of my teachers. I knew I was a whiz at the rosary, a relatively devout kid with a well-developed sense of guilt, speedy at the Scriptures and could pull a one-second flat kneel-and-pray move that was the envy of my peers.

My first official recruiting visit began when Brother Driscoll, our art teacher, slipped me a note after class, instructing me to meet him at the Brothers' entrance. The Brothers lived at the school - in fact, they built the entire thing, and they thrived on recruiting kids like me to join them. Fresh from the high school ranks, 18-year old boys would attend St. John's University in Queens for free while living with the Brothers at the school, preparing for a life of teaching and handyman work, until four years later when, with a degree in religion in one hand and a new tool belt in the other, these young men would enter the celibate religious life forever, teaching, praying and regrouting.

I did what I was told and waited outside the entrance as instructed. Even though I knew I was a sought-after soul, I really had no idea why I was getting the call now. Maybe this had nothing to do with recruiting. Maybe they knew I'd cut class a few weeks before to go to the beach with my girlfriend, but that forged note was a masterful fake, wasn't it? Did they discover I always ate lunch with John, the kid who stole bags of merchandise from the school store while everyone else was at First Friday Mass? He bragged about it out loud to anyone who'd listen, and I never turned him in. Oh no! Was I going down for not being a rat? Maybe I wasn't such a solid Catholic after all. The minutes ticked by and panic began to set in when, just before I fell to my knees to confess my sins, the door opened and Brother Driscoll greeted me with a huge smile.

He led me down a Minotaur's maze of halls, the walls covered with the Stations of the Cross or Dogs Playing Poker - or a combination of the two – my hyperventilating was so distracting that I couldn't tell the difference. The hallways went on forever, and I started to wish I'd saved my gummi bears from lunch to leave a trail, like little Hansel, if things took an ugly turn. I half-expected to wake up with the vague taste of chloroform on my lips, a sore backside, and a bus token in an alley in Long Island City, but Brother Driscoll kept it above board, and he led me into a sitting room where I learned the true nature of my visit.

"Timothy," Brother Driscoll began, "have you ever considered joining us here in religious life? We think you have what it takes to be a member of this community. You'll start by spending the summer in Appalachia clearing brush and praying. Then you'll return here to the school where you'll help us replace the carpet in the Earth Science lab and apply wax sealant on the new toilets in the locker rooms, followed by more praying."

After that offer, the only praying I wanted to do was praying like hell I never had to pick up a single twig in the backwoods of West Virginia. "No thanks, Brother. I have plans for the summer," I explained, ending my one and only recruiting visit for life after high school. No booster dollars, no immoral cheerleader visits, and no name on the scoreboard for the full effect. I'm sure I could have had a few novenas said in my honor if I'd pressed my luck, but Brother Driscoll had landscapes to paint and quotas to fill, so I found my way out to freedom, a life of religious devotion and yard work rejected.

Turning down a scholarship and a starting spot on the Landscapin' Eunuchs may have given Jesus reason to let our bond weaken, but I know we can get things back on track if he'd put some effort into fielding the right team. But that's not enough. I'm okay with my boyfriend's image showing up on every other grilled cheese, veggie burrito and deep-dish pizza crust across the land, but I am not okay with him looking so miserable all the time. I can't tell for certain if Jesus has wooden teeth, but even if he does, I need a man who isn't afraid to flash those chompers, be they pearly white or knotty pine.

Turning that frown upside down would do wonders for Jesus' public image. He'd become the Man of the Hour the moment someone spied his face in a chalupa, giving the double-guns slick-guy salute or smiling as he flips the bird, twin-barrel style. Jesus can put his likeness on anything he wants, so why shouldn't he make himself more exciting? The crucial 18-to-35 demographic can't be ignored, and what better way to say, "Follow me to eternal salvation!" than Jesus flashing the heavy metal horns on an Eggo Waffle? The possibilities are infinite.

The next time a devout loner makes the news holding a half-eaten Salisbury steak with the image of God Almighty's son on it, Jesus could be nailing a fakie-to-forward 1080 in a mountainside half-pipe, or dropping into the green room off Waikiki, or maybe even dressed as Obi Wan fighting Anakin Skywalker with a simple shepherd's light saber. With Jesus as the sketch artist, we'd wait like Franklin Mint collectors for the next appearance, never knowing what he was up to next. The buzz would be palpable, and Jesus would be back on top, feeling great about himself and ready to commit to our love as an equal partner.

There's no doubt my relationship with Jesus is complicated. All I'm asking for is some effort on the other guy's part. Like my daughter, I could use a little more Jesus in my heart and in my lunch as well. It's tough making a long-distance relationship work, and I'm hoping Jesus embraces my suggestions so we can stick together and be happy forever. So until he returns my calls, I'll continue to wait. I'll be the one sitting in the corner, eating my soft tacos, waiting for my man to come around.

GOODBYE, GRAMMAR GEEK

Between you and I, good grammar is for losers. This, of course, means you're a loser if you read that first sentence and noticed something amiss. Fear not – your secret's safe with me. I've been a total loser most of my life – a grammar geek, to be honest – so you're among friends. Well, you were until the other day when I decided to ditch my obsession with the rules of the written and spoken word for an existence no longer slavish to all things grammatically correct.

The reason for this drastic change of heart is simple – no one else seems to care, so why should I? I don't want to end up like an old Japanese soldier on a remote island in the South Pacific, running in circles yelling "Banzai" and waving a palm frond sword at the Discovery Channel cameraman while everyone else stands around smirking, wondering why no one told him the fight ended decades ago. I have no desire to find myself, fifty years from now, standing in the middle of Times Square, brandishing my dog-eared copy of Strunk and White, barking about the virtues of the semicolon while the crowd just winks and smiles, never bothering to tell me the President signed an executive order decades before, outlawing all unnecessary complicated punctuation across the land "To protect the sanctity of instant messaging and for the good of the nation."

The bitter memory of a semicolon incident from my past is reason enough to move on with my life. I was thirteen, at summer camp, sitting around with my friends waiting for the mail. As it arrived, my friend Rob opened a letter from his dad and began reading. "My dad is a total loser!" Rob yelled. "He used semicolons in this letter! What kind of a dork even knows what a semicolon is?"

Rob roared as the group laughed along, apparently united in the belief that only dorky dads use them to link independent clauses not joined by a coordinating conjunction, further ignoring the reality so clear in my teenage brain that semicolons should join only those independent clauses that are closely related in meaning. But

I said nothing, offering the poor piece of punctuation no help as it was crushed under the cruel boot of teenaged anti-grammatical hostility. From that day on, I knew I was different. I cared about grammar.

Blame it on my parents, my teachers in Catholic school or maybe even *Schoolhouse Rock.* I was a committed grammarphile. I thought gerunds were groovy, knew that genitive cases could not be cured with Penicillin, and I believed the transitive/intransitive verb debate was one of high stakes and intense drama.

Minutes after hearing the song "Karma Chameleon" for the first time in high school, I thought about how witty it would be to change the title to "Comma Chameleon." I imagined singing it to my English teacher, Brother Harold, for extra credit, showing him I was doing more than just paying attention – I was *living* the grammar he taught us. "Writing would be easy if you added your commas with ease, with grace and ease . . ." the lyrics went, and I thought it was brilliant.

Just before I shared this erudite gem, I caught a glimpse of my classmate, Terry, standing behind me. Terry was one of the many classmates of mine who could sniff out the smart kids to menace with ease. Not only was it a bad idea to be seen chatting with the teacher, but chatting about grammar was, in Terry's eyes, grounds for an immediate clobbering. Add that to the fact that I was seconds away from busting loose an impersonation of Boy George, and we had a serious facial reconstruction in the making.

I chose to hide my light under a bushel of fear that day, which may have saved me. I knew what Terry was capable of. He'd spent most of the previous Saturday copying every one of my answers to the verbal section of the SAT college entrance exam. I knew this because his prodigious hominid brow cast a gloomy pall over my answer sheet all morning. He cornered me as we left the exam room, asking, "Your good at English and shit, right?" I could hear the missing apostrophe in his voice but decided to nod slowly and not make any sudden movements for fear I'd upset the delicate balance of 7-11 Cola Slurpee and wet cement that made up the majority of Terry's frontal lobe.

I spent hours in high school hoping I'd be the subject of my own After School Special, *Too Young to Conjugate*. A dreamy Rob Lowe would play me, and Helen Hunt would be my best friend, love interest and sentence-diagramming partner in the state tournament. We'd take the abuse at school from the kids who loved to mock us, but deep down wanted to despise dangling modifiers as much as we did. Helen and I would come home to my house where my mom would leave a snack and her Supreme Court legal briefs on the kitchen table for me to edit while Helen told me how she suspected her dad could only read at a fourth-grade level.

"But he loves you. That's all that matters," I'd say, my mind deep in a solution involving subordinate clauses in the past perfect tense. My assurances would ring hollow with Helen, and she'd notice the slight contempt in my voice. We'd fight just before making up and winning at States, beating James Spader, the snobby kid with kick-ass restrictive appositive instincts from Valley Central, in the dramatic final showdown.

My obsession with grammar permeated most aspects of my life. I couldn't listen to the radio without noticing the transgressions. I gave in and cried when Paul McCartney sang "But if this ever-changing world in which we live in, makes you give in and cry," and Jerry Lee Lewis singing "Breathless" made me just that. It puzzled me that no one seemed to notice the error when the Killer sang, "Ah come on baby, now don't be shy - This love was meant for you and I."

Didn't anyone realize, including everyone else who also married their twelve-year-old cousin, that Jerry Lee was using a subject pronoun incorrectly? Any bumpkin with a thimble dose of book learnin' knows a pronoun that follows a preposition must be an *object* pronoun. I wanted to send him a corrected version that read, "Ah come on baby, why won't you listen to me? Using object pronouns will set you free . . . ." But I decided against it, imagining Jerry Lee and his child bride giggling hysterically while tossing my letter into a backyard bonfire as they guzzled sour mash moonshine from dirty mason jars.

I'm excited not to be tied down by the shackles of long-ignored rules any longer. No more will I care where a period goes - inside or outside the quotation mark is fine by me, and I'll tell anyone who'll listen that the semicolon is just Morse code for morons. I promise not to bristle when I hear friends say things like, "Me and him are gonna break your head if you correct us one more time." And now my life's goal is to encourage the universal spelling of the contraction **it's** as "its," knowing its wrong but feeling like its a lost cause.

Yes, its true. I don't give two shits about its anymore, and it feels so good. In fact, just yesterday, at my local Friendly's restaurant, I noticed my placemat had the word calendar misspelled as "calandar," and I didn't even point it out to the wait staff! I kept on eating my ise kream without a kare in the world. Let's face it, its a krazy, kandy-kolored, pressure-kooker world out there, and the less time we spend worrying about the rules, the more time we'll have to live life to the most fullest. Take it from myself, say goodbye to the grammar geek inside you and embrace that little piece of Terry that lurks within. Trust me - you'll be happier, have more time to rock out, and you might even do good on your SATs this time around.

FEEL THE WEASEL

Describing what it feels like to pass a kidney stone for someone who's never had one is like trying to explain a two-beer buzz to a Mormon – it loses something in the translation. And so goes it with kidney stones – unless you've crawled around on the bathroom floor of a Mexican restaurant wincing in misery or wept openly like Nancy Kerrigan in front of a room full of adults, you can't really imagine it.

The pain sneaks up on you like a plumbing problem in the kitchen. One day you're watching the water hesitate before heading down the drain, vaguely remembering your brother apologizing for cramming an avocado pit down the disposal, and the next day, you're ankle- deep in fetid sewage, begging the plumber to come quick, swearing off guacamole forever. It may start as a trickle, but when kidney stones arrive, the misery corkscrews its way through you like that plumber's drain snake covered in thumb tacks.

I'm one of the lucky few who's had more than one stone to pass, and not knowing what was wrong the first time, I went to a doctor. I found the office just down the street from my apartment and saw a man standing inside, smoking a cigarette and wearing a sweaty tee shirt, his hair thinning and wild atop his head. Figuring I'd interrupted a pipe fitter on his union break, I turned to go when the man called out, "Are you my 12:15? Come on in and grab a seat."

"Wonderful," I said to myself. "I'm starting to feel a disturbance in my delicate man area, and this guy looks like he just used a claw hammer to install a drainage pipe in the basement." I introduced myself and we sat down, a strong scent of body odor, stale smoke and Aqua Velva surrounding us.

"What's wrong, young fella?" the doctor began. Having no idea, I started to explain that my pee pee felt funny – that it was kind of burning and uncomfortable. The doctor stared at me, smiled as smoke curled over his beaded lip, and asked me if I was married. "You know, a new married guy like you, playing around with the ladies – you can get any kind of disease. Lemme take a look," he said as he put his cigarette out and grabbed the rubber gloves. Thirty seconds later I was bent over his table, the doctor's fingers exploring my nether regions as the smell of menthol Kools and cheap aftershave wafted through the air. I was so surprised by the insinuation that I had a case of the clap I didn't have much time to resist the prostate massage.

Finding nothing, he warned me to keep an eye on myself, and if I started running a fever, I needed to get some VD pills pronto – "and I can call it in for you – no sense letting the wife know, you know?" He smiled at me in a sort of creepy, let's-go-check-out-the-peephole-in-the-ladies-room kind of way. I thanked him for his time and beat it out of there like a cheating husband racing home to make curfew.

Still no wiser, I fell asleep that night wondering if I'd caught VD from a toilet seat. I woke up a few hours later, shooting out of bed and onto the floor. The pain was unbelievable. On a scale of one to ten, with ten the worst pain imaginable, I'd rate it a thirty-seven, enough to force me into my wife's closet, where I started gnawing on a leather clog to stop me from swallowing my tongue. But just as quickly as it started, the pain was gone, disappeared – no explanation, no reason, nothing.

A few years passed, and I never gave that brief interlude much thought, although the smell of Aqua Velva did give me a lingering sense of shame. The second stone arrived like the first. This time, a dour, young female doctor wasted no time telling me that Chlamydia was easy to cure. When I explained that my wife and I were happily married, she looked down, embarrassed by my apparent lies, and told me to come back once the lab tests confirmed my social disease. Why a 5'5" chubby guy gives off the vibe of a two-timing skirt-chasing lothario is beyond me, but I decided to tackle that situation another day. In the meantime, things were percolating down below, and I was getting nervous.

It was St. Patrick's Day – my wife's birthday – and we went out with friends to a Mexican restaurant in Cambridge, Mass. The meal, the beers, the conversation were all lovely, but when I went to the bathroom and stood at the urinal, it felt like someone had stabbed me in the lower back with a frozen chimichanga, and I fell to my knees. Good to know the fine male citizens of Cambridge run at the sight of a whimpering man in the bathroom, all of them slithering away as if St. Paddy himself was casting them out. I managed to get up, get back to the table and convince my wife to skip the birthday cake and drive me home. Rest assured, nothing says "Happy Birthday" to a grown woman like a crying husband holding his wiener and screaming for help.

En route, we called the doctor, who told me either to go home and drink water until the stone passed or to get to the hospital for medication. I chose the water-torture method, but after twenty minutes, I pleaded with my wife to take me to the ER. The pain had moved from my lower back to my special area, and it was relentless, like a non-stop wave of the sensation you get when you stub your little toe on the bedpost over and over again, except it's not your toe you're stubbing.

The rest of the night was a blur. I remember crawling around on the floor of the ER waiting room, taking Vicodin for the first time, and bawling like an infant when the first shot didn't work. I have a hazy recollection of the nurse shaking her head in disappointment as I cried for my mommy.

The next day, to confirm I'd passed the stone in my dope-induced stupor, the doctors told me to swing by the office to prep for x-rays and that they had something waiting for me. Wee! Pony stickers for a Super Patient! Instead, I got a bag of enemas. Four of them. I guess crying jags, hobbling around on all fours in public and suspicion of infidelity weren't enough. Maybe these doctors wanted to punish me for weeping like that, figuring if I could bawl like a baby, I should be forced to control my bowels like one. I will share no more of the following twenty-four hours of that ordeal, except to say that when one is asked to take a course of enemas, one should remain as close to one's bathroom as possible.

Just recently, in the early morning hours of Labor Day, I dreamed an enraged Viking stood on my bed. He wore a horned helmet, and his massive frame was draped with animal skins while juices from plundered mutton dripped down his chin. The Viking wore size sixteen ski boots and vengefully worked his right heel into my groin, and it hurt a lot. I woke up, but Ragnar the Berserker was nowhere to be found – I was alone with this pain, no Viking in sight. The stones were back.

This odyssey began with a trip to the urologist, confirming the offender's location deep in my body's recesses, the stone a tiny white blip on the ultrasound, and the doctor talking about my urethra like we'd skipped dinner, drinks, and dancing and moved right into baby-making.

She ushered me out of her office, and as I gingerly walked toward the door, I scanned a wall of pamphlets filled with a wide selection of reading material on lots of nasty situations like "Fixing Leaking Bladders" and "Un-Herniating Your Testicles." Finally, I found one titled, "Understanding Kidney Stones."

Understanding kidney stones? I already *understood* all I needed – kidney stones were as fun as a bag of angry spiders. While the other pamphlets showed loving families huddled together on grandma's pee-soaked afghan or Dad salsa dancing with his children in his post-op gown, I got a ten-page book about how kidney stones hurt real bad, with such headings as "Management for a Lifetime," and "The Pain You'll Never Forget." Tell me about it.

The cover said it all: a man stands on a golf course, holding his side with a look of intense anguish on his face. No hugging families here – not even a supporting golfing buddy offering a hand. His foursome must have driven the cart away at high speeds leaving their buddy to fend for himself, fearing he'd either detonate or drive his putter into their eye sockets to stop the misery. The man's face looks like some sort of woodland creature is attacking him – like an angry weasel chewing on his privates. I thought back to those hours in the ER, and that's exactly what this felt like - a long, continuous clench and grind of sharp tiny teeth against my defenseless and paper-thin man membrane. This guy was feeling the weasel.

I knew the brutal truth: my time would soon arrive. The doctor reminded me that the pain was uncomfortable now, but as the stone made its move from my bladder to my urethra and then onto freedom, I'd go from mild discomfort to intense agony to unbearable, psychotic, incoherent torment. By the end, I'd be praying for Erik the Red's nephew to pillage me just to distract me from the pain. At this point, a leaking bladder sounded so much more fun.

I then did the only thing a semi-coherent wimp who knew what was coming would do – I fueled up on pain killers like a Led Zeppelin roadie on payday. As the weasel got closer and closer, I fought him off with fistfuls of Percocet and Vicodin - the Goofus and Gallant of the pain killer set. I also washed down a mouthful of Advil with a tureen of cheap red wine - all of this advised by my doctor, whose last words to me were, "And if none of that works, get someone to drive you to the ER."

The drugs did nothing to thwart the weasel's relentless approach. I was now entering the zone where you lose all sense of time and space; you're left to rock back and forth, trying to find any kind of trance to stop the insanity.

So as I swayed to and fro in my kitchen, my children recoiled at the sight of their glassy-eyed father moving like a huge drugged-out human metronome. Finally, as the pain progressed, I got to the hospital.

My advice to you, if ever confronted with a long line at the hospital, is to scrunch your face up, walk like you're ninety-five years old and mutter two simple words – "kidney stone." The ER staff, the nurses, even the other patients, will run for cover, giving you instant access to a bed, an IV and lots of "poor guy" comments uttered with genuine concern.

Despite having enough substances coursing through my bloodstream to qualify me for a starting spot on the all-drug Olympic team, the ER staff wasted no time pumping me full of more. Minutes after arriving, the nurse approached me with a syringe that must have come from a circus vet's medicine bag. It was filled with Dilaudid, and the nurse smiled and told me in a few moments I'd feel nothing. She hit me with the needle, and all my cares didn't evaporate – they, along with any emotion or unique idea I'd ever had, bolted from my brain, drowned in a sea of prescribed narcotics. Twenty seconds later I felt nothing – not the unrelenting pain in my crotch, not the sharp arcs of turmoil in my backside, not even my feet touching the floor.

Finally, the weasel, the Viking, the torture were all gone in the push of a pencil-sized needle, replaced by a numb, zombie-like quality that won me no favors at home for the next two days, considering I spent them either asleep or drooling in front of the TV.

As George Harrison once suggested, all things must pass, and this whopper of a stone did, a few days after my drugstore cowboy rodeo ride. It left with little fanfare, landing in the toilet bowl with an almost-audible "plink" as it headed down the drain and out of my life for good.

But I know it's not over, because somewhere, in my not-too-distant future, I see a Viking, ferociously laughing as he buckles up his ski boots, his pet weasel tugging frantically at his leather whip leash, a crazy look in his eyes. They're planning their next attack, and my only hope is that I can hold back the tears until the drugs kick in.

THE TIME OF YOUR LIFE

I stood on the long, curved concourse of Nassau Coliseum, my friends next to me as the crowd surged past. I clutched my first concert ticket in my hand, a Kinks ticket, my thirteen-year-old face doing its best to hide the fact that I was scared to death. I'd seen *Gimme Shelter* twice already, and I waited for the Hells Angels to pounce from the shadows, knowing they'd smell my fear like they'd sniff out the Undercover Fuzz at a drug sale. Or worse - what if someone forced me to take drugs? I'd heard some people never came home from Woodstock. Would I become a runaway? Or maybe I'd make it home safe only to lead a life of vacant confusion, an endless loop of "Lola" playing in my addled brain as I stood in line for food stamps.

But the ticket in my hand trumped that fear – I was witnessing live music from a band I'd only seen on album covers, and I couldn't wait. I started walking to my seat when a teenager moved in a blur past me, brushing my shoulder as he ran by, not noticing the enormous puddle of beer-soaked vomit on the floor. The running teen slipped, flew up in the air, and landed directly into the middle of the brownish sludge, falling back into it as the crowd laughed and groaned with better-him-than-me glee. This is what I remember most about my first rock concert.

Twenty-five years later, with that image still clear in my mind, I bought two tickets for me and my ten-year-old son to see Green Day. Telling him, I expected a high-five and a mad dash upstairs to start working on the entire Green Day catalogue on his electric guitar. Instead, Sam greeted my announcement of tickets with, "Um, will there be people smoking and fighting?"

The concert approached, and Sam's anxiety increased – "How loud will it be? Will we be too close to the stage? Do you know how to get there?" Sam asked me this as we shared a Capri Sun and a bag of popcorn, not quite the same as a cold malt liquor and a handful of 'luudes, but then again, this was his first concert.

We approached the arena, and the questions continued. "Dad, do you have the tickets? Can I see them? Are you sure they are for this concert? Will the lines be really long?" We got in line, and Sam spied a fellow 4th grader from town, each giving furtive waves of recognition.

The kid's dad looked me over, probably thinking, "What kind of moron takes a ten-year-old to a Green Day show?" Exactly, my friend – see you in the mosh pit.

We took our seats in the Van Allen Belt section near the catwalk, our eyes growing cloudy from the lack of oxygen. My Chemical Romance, the opening band, began the show, and immediately, the lead singer screamed, "Are you motherfuckers ready to rock this fucking house?"

Perfect! My son was already convinced he was taking attendance at a parolee picnic, and the first words he hears are enough to give his straight-laced heart palpitations. Sam muttered to me above the potty-talk din, "Why does he have to use language like that! I mean *really!*" The longer My Chemical Romance played, the more Sam started to remind me of Sylvester the Cat's son – "Oh Father, I am so disappointed in you." I tried to explain that artists need to feel free to express themselves however they want. "Well, the artists *I* know don't need to use so many bad words," Sam scowled as he sat back in his seat.

The set ended, and as we waited for Green Day, a large pink rabbit stumbled onstage with a pawful of beers, dancing a drunken jig for the crowd. People howled as the enormous bunny chugged half a six-pack, hopping and skipping as he downed each beer. Sam, not sure what to make of this semi-cosmic interlude, glanced at me with a look that said, "There's still time to make a run for it!" Then the lights went out, and the place absolutely erupted. Green Day sprinted onstage, launching into "American Idiot" as everyone went bananas.

The ensuing two hours were a mixture of intense live music and lots of nervous complaining. "Dad, sit down! Oh my God, Dad, you're embarrassing me! Please Dad stop! You're being so weird!" It could have been a lot weirder if I'd gone into my standard concert-going mode of cheap booze, tobacco-related smoking products, and careless, dance-fueled sweating, but I kept it safe and sane for the boy's sake – no need to see Daddy slipping in a puddle of his own puke as he chants along to "Welcome to Paradise."

I started to wonder if my son was going Amish on me. He should have been leaping from his seat and pumping his arms at every beat of "Geek Stink Breath," but Sam just sat there. I half-expected a lecture from him - "Your whirling arm movements, although reminiscent of Uncle Yacob's wheat thresher on the farm, frighten and confuse me, wayward father. Spirit me home for evening prayers with alacrity."

Lucky for me, Green Day marched on, and Sam began to warm up. The great music, tons of energy, strobe lights, confetti cannons, and lots of fist-pumping, arm-waving, lyric-chanting fans were too much for him to ignore. In the end he was powerless to resist the lure of live rock and roll. When the lead singer, Billie Joe, asked if any guitar players in the crowd wanted to join him onstage, Sam immediately raised his hand, and for that one brief instant, Sam joined the fellowship of rock concert goers, letting go of whatever was convincing him life without live music was a life worth living. I smiled and raised my hand too.

The band left the stage, and we started to run out, but we heard more and ran back inside to see Billie Joe sing, "Good Riddance (Time of your Life)" by himself, a spotlight blazing down on him center-stage, the delirious, exhausted crowd singing along to every word, waving their arms in unison. We stood next to each other in the darkness as the music pulsed through us, connecting us to the song, the experience and to one another.

For weeks after the show, I wondered if Sam had had enough fun to ever want to go back, if he'd been bitten by the bug like I'd been so long ago. Then I heard him humming the refrain from "Good Riddance." He didn't know I listened as he sang under his breath, "I hope you had the time of your life," and I thought, this *IS* your life, Sam - filled with noise, chaos, pushing, screaming, careening six-foot drunken rabbits and a dad who just wants to dance and sing at the top of his lungs. This is what life gives you - and it's worth every note. So listen up. And look out for the vomit.